ne night, years ago, my wife and I were walking along the beach in Venice, California when we came upon the bones of the old Venice Pier. The struts, tracks, and ties of the ancient roller-coaster were strewn down the shore, collapsed in the tides.

"What," I asked, "is that dinosaur's skeleton doing, lying here on the sand?"

From that encounter, I wrote The Beast from Twenty Thousand Fathoms, *the story of a dinosaur who falls in love with a fog horn in a light house.*

At dinner some years later, the president of a television network suddenly turned to me and said:

"If I gave you a million dollars and prime time, what kind of show would you do?"

"Dinosaurs!" I cried, without hesitation. "Dinosaurs!"

Thus illustrating once again my constant love for those prehistoric wonders.

But the fact is, we all *love dinosaurs!*

There isn't a man, woman or child in the world who, if I built it, wouldn't rush to climb in a Time Machine to jump back and be devoured by your Tyrannosaurus Rex or stomped on by your friendly local Brontosaurus. The devouring and stomping would be accidental, of course. We would mainly go to see, gasp at, and love those mighty beauties. It would be worth taking a chance on winding up as the beasts' primeval breakfast.

Well now, here's that very Machine. This book, by William Stout, William Service and Byron Preiss, travels you wonderously in Time and lands you where you've always wanted to be: cheek by jowl with the mighty samurai lizards, striding through a jungle that goes on forever, or hang-gliding with live nightmare kites in a Lost Hour that will never end.

I've already been there, and it's grand.

Now, it's your turn. Open the book. Travel.

Love the Beasts.

—Ray Bradbury

THE
DINOSAURS

ILLUSTRATED BY
WILLIAM STOUT

NARRATED BY
WILLIAM SERVICE

EDITED BY
BYRON PREISS

INTRODUCTION AND
SCIENTIFIC COMMENTARY BY
DR. PETER DODSON
UNIVERSITY OF PENNSYLVANIA
SCIENTIFIC CONSULTANT

A
Byron Preiss
Book

MALLARD
PRESS

For Barry Denenberg, who took it personally
—B.P.

For Pegge

—W. Service

For Eliot Wittenberg, my fifth grade teacher,
the man who first encouraged my art with an
attitude that gave it importance. One person
can make a difference.

—W. Stout

Acknowledgements

William Stout wishes to acknowledge the following special people for their very generous support, patience and assistance: Kent Wilson, Byron Preiss, William Service, Dr. Peter Dodson, Alex Jay, Robert A. Long, George Olshevsky, Sylvia Massey, Donald F. Glut, The Dinosaur Society of Los Angeles, Joyce Sommers, Judy Goode, Alison Buckles and Lucy Knight Steele. Special thanks to Rob Cobb, John Milius and Buzz Feitshans —a true A-TEAM.

The Author wishes to thank Joe Rees for his tireless research and assistance.

The Editor wishes to thank Mr. Louis Wolfe, for his personal commitment to *The Dinosaurs;* Stephen Weitzen, for the new edition; Edmund Preiss, our attorney; Pearl Preiss; Joan Brandt; Sydny Weinberg; and Sandi Mendelson. Special thanks to Ian and Betty Ballantine, for their friendship and for their pioneering work in the field.

This book was produced by Byron Preiss Visual Publications, Inc.,
24 West 25th Street, New York, New York 10010.

The cover and book design were done by Alex Jay, who developed
and designed a new display typeface for the interior titles of
the book, inspired in part by letterforms in Alphonse Mucha's classic
1901 Art Nouveau portfolio, Documents Decoratifs.

The cover illustration by William Stout expresses the style Art Dino
(art dee-no), an illustrative and decorative approach inspired
by the naturalist art of Charles R. Knight, Zdenek Burian, and
the Detmold Brothers; the decorative art of Art Nouveau designers
such as Alphonse Mucha; and the fantastic art of Arthut Rackham,
N.C. Wyeth and Frank Frazetta.

Library of Congress Cataloging in Publication Data

Stout, William, 1949–
The Dinosaurs
1. Dinosaurs. I. Preiss, Byron.
II. Service, William. 1930– III. Title
QE 862.D5S73   567.9'1   81-2655
ISBN 0-792-45357-3

Published by MALLARD PRESS
An Imprint of BDD Promotional Book Company, Inc.
666 Fifth Avenue
New York, New York 10103
Mallard Press and its accompanying design and logo are
trademarks of BDD Promotional Book Company, Inc.

PRINTED IN ITALY

0 9 8 7 6 5 4 3 2 1

INTRODUCTION

by Dr. Peter Dodson

In the 157 years since their discovery, dinosaurs have exerted an almost magical fascination on the public. Visitors who flock to the dinosaur halls of our great natural history museums stand in awe of the bulk and sheer size of the complete skeletons that gaze dumbly down at them. Childhood memories harbor cherished images of lumbering brontosaurs wading around in swamps. Cartoons, movies, children's books—even many educational ones —perpetuate outmoded notions. From them we are tempted to conclude that dinosaurs were nearly static creatures and that the study of dinosaurs is similarly static. Nothing could be farther from the truth. The study of dinosaurs has undergone a great renaissance in recent years. About 250 *genera* (kinds) of dinosaurs have received valid names since the first were described in 1824; fully 20% (50 kinds) of these have been since 1970; the previous record for naming new dinosaurs was during the 1920's, when 30 were named. Corresponding with this feverish activity on the part of paleontologists—the students of fossils of ancient life—new concepts have emerged concerning the appearance, activities, behavior, social structure, mating habits and nesting of dinosaurs; in short, our entire concept of these admirable creatures has been altered.

Clearly this book is not a text in dinosaur biology; neither is in an exercise in science fiction. Rather it is an attempt to revitalize dinosaurs and to draw upon the new scientific insights that have emerged in the past decade, in order to reconstruct the world in which the dinosaurs lived, and to portray, in a plausible manner, how these animals realis-

tically would have behaved on a daily basis, how they dealt with the situations that they encountered each day, how they interacted with members their own kind and with members of other species. The poetic license that has created a dramatic narrative has been tempered by facts, reasonable inference and restrained speculation.

The scientific understanding of dinosaurs has been greatly aided by casting off the notion that dinosaurs were merely overgrown lizards. Models of dinosaur activity are no longer constrained by what reptiles look like or do today because lizards, snakes and especially turtles are only distantly related to dinosaurs. Only crocodilians, a mere handful of very similar species today, are close reptilian cousins of dinosaurs; and their short legs and aquatic, predatory habits are very unlike those of most dinosaurs. To understand dinosaurs, it is useful to consider as well the living animals that most resemble them in size and food habits: the large mammals, such as the elephant and the rhinoceros. Much more is known about the ecology and behavior of these mammals than was the case in the past, and thus the current interpretation of dinosaurs has a sounder biological basis than was the case in the past.

Withal, dinosaurs were unique: they were not overgrown lizards; neither were they African mammals. The paleontologist Walter P. Coombs Jr. epitomizes the question clearly in his thoughts about the sauropods, the brontosaurus-like dinosaurs: "What can be said of the habits of a creature with the nose of a *Macrauchenia* (an extinct South American mammal), the neck of a giraffe, the limbs of an elephant, the feet of a chalicothere (an extinct relative of the horse), the lungs of a

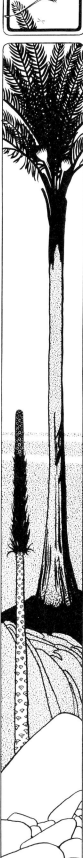

bird and the tail of a lizard? With so many plausible but conflicting interpretations, it is unlikely there will be general agreement on sauropod habits as long as more than one paleontologist has an opinion on the matter." So much more if the name "sauropod" be changed to the more general "dinosaur"!

Who Were The Dinosaurs?

Dinosaurs lived from the Late Triassic Period, some 200 million years ago, through the Jurassic Period lasting to 140 million years ago, until the end of the Cretaceous Period, ending about 63 million years ago. They constituted the dominant forms of life on earth for nearly 140 million years. Although they are now extinct, in no way can they be considered "failures". Dinosaurs are popularly thought to be any large reptile during the Age of Reptiles or Mesozoic Era. This is not the case. Many creatures attained large size during those lush, warm, benign and halcyon days: crocodiles may have reached fifty feet in length, long-necked plesiosaurs and thirty foot mosasaurs plied the seas to the detriment of the fishy denizens, and a cousin of today's little sardine reached twelve feet in length.

Like turtles, snakes and lizards, the abundant reptiles of today's world, dinosaurs had dry, scaley skin, and a certain general organization of skull, jaws and skeleton. Dinosaurs shared with crocodiles a skull with two sets of openings in the cheek bones behind the eye, teeth set in sockets, and a certain structure of bones that surround the brain. A great cohort of reptiles, the subclass called the *Archosaurs* or "ruling reptiles," possessed these characteristics and differed from all others of the reptilian class. During the Triassic, there was a great variety of archosaurs, some rabbit-sized, some cow-sized; some clumsy, some swift; some terrestrial, some semi-aquatic, some highly-aquatic; some heavily armored. Most were four-legged, but a few thecodonts—the dinosaurs' ancestors—discovered a better idea: walking about on hind legs. By the end of the Triassic, a sorting-out of archosaurs had occurred, "experimental types" disappeared, and the "successes" emerged: crocodiles, flying reptiles (pterosaurs) and the dinosaurs. Crocodiles alone survive today, but what a success the dinosaurs enjoyed during their allotted time!

Dinosaurs (the name means "terrible lizard") differed from all other archosaurs by a special structure of the hip and the ankle which facilitated swift upright movement. In 1841, the famous British anatomist Sir Richard Owen coined the name "dinosaur" to encompass an *order* of giant extinct reptiles. Some years later, in 1887, Harry Groves Seeley recognized that Owen's order actually consisted of two quite separate orders, distinguished on the basis of pelvic structure. The pelvis of members of the *Order Saurischia* resembled that of lizards in a general way; the pelvis of the *Order Ornithischia* resembled that of birds. Saurischians included both meat-eaters (carnivores) and plant-eaters (herbivores): all ornithischians were plant-eaters.

In saurischian dinosaurs, one rod of bone, the pubis, pointed downward from the hip joint, and another pointed downward and backward, the ischium. Three designs of body build were found among the saurischians. The *prosauropods,* such as *Plateosaurus* or *Ammosaurus,* were of small to moderate size, not exceeding 20 feet in length, and were confined to the earliest part of the age of dinosaurs. They were ungraceful-looking plant-eaters that spent part of their time on four feet and part of their time with their short, stocky forefeet off the ground. The *sauropods* included brontosaurus (properly known as *Apatosaurus), Diplodocus* and friends. These largest of dinosaurs had long necks and tails and small heads. These small-brained, inoffensive herbivores were common during only the middle part of the Age of Reptiles. Although they survived until the end, in most places in the Northern hemisphere they were displaced by more advanced ornithischians of much smaller size. *Theropods* constituted the third group of saurischians and the only group of flesh-eaters. *Tyrannosaurus rex,* the two-legged creature with long tail, short forelimbs and neck, huge head and menacing teeth was the largest of the theropods. *Tyrannosaurus* lived at the very end of the Age of Reptiles, but in every known dinosaur community some smaller theropod with those general predatory attributes existed. In many dinosaur communities there were both large and small theropods, just as mammalian communities may have wolves, foxes and weasels. Theropods ranged in size down to the turkey-sized *Compsognathus.*

Ornithischian dinosaurs were all herbivores, and there were four body plans for them. *Ornithopods* were two-legged types who appeared at the beginning of the Age of Reptiles as small-tusked animals *(Heterodontosaurus)* and persisted through the Era, giving rise to the Cretaceous giant, *Iguanodon* and to the duck-billed hadrosaurs. *Hadrosaurs* had the most elaborate teeth of any dinosaurs, and many had showy crests of various shapes on their heads. *Stegosaurs* were bulky four-footed herbivores famous for their small heads and the distinctive triangular plates on their backs. Rather weak teeth may have limited these herbivores' existence to the Jurassic Period. *Ankylosaurs* were the archaic herbivores of the Cretaceous, preserving the small relative brain size and simple tooth pattern of their predecessors. These broad, low, animals were heavily armored on their backs and heads, and some dragged a bony tail club. Small weak teeth limited their effectiveness as herbivores. *Ceratopsians,* or horned dinosaurs of the Late Cretaceous (the final phase of the Age of Reptiles), were rhinoceros-like animals with various combinations of horns over eye and nose and elaborate bony frills that covered portions of the neck and chest. Their elaborate teeth were second only to the duck-bills' in effectiveness.

The World of the Dinosaurs

The world in which the dinosaurs lived looked very different from our modern world. Early in the Age of Reptiles, all of the continents were joined together into one great landmass, Pangaea. The Atlantic Ocean simply did not exist. Nor did great mountain ranges tower over the Mesozoic plains: the Alps, Rockies, Andes and Himalayas were yet to come. About 200 million years ago, the great landmass began to breakup; slowly North America began to drift westward and northward. Near the end of the Age of Dinosaurs, it was close to the position it occupies today, but split in two by a seaway that extended from the Arctic Ocean to the Gulf of Mexico. The Atlantic Ocean lapped on the shore of Philadelphia, Florida did not exist, and the Gulf of Mexico came up the Mississippi as far as Missouri. The joining and sundering of continents, the rise and fall of mountains, the spread and

waning of seas had great effect on dinosaur distribution. At times they could walk between Europe and North America; at other times between North America and Asia. Dinosaurs are known from all continents except Antartica and it is likely they will be found there, too. Remains have been found in the Canadian Yukon and on the Arctic island, Spitzbergen. The climates of the Mesozoic were generally much warmer than today's north temperate climate, even in today's Arctic. Although dinosaurs thrived in lush, wet, warm climates, as exemplified by the rich fossil beds of western Canada and of Tanzania in eastern Africa, they successfully endured seasonal dryness in the American west and aridity in Mongolia.

Size and Its Consequences

Dinosaur afficionados have wanted their dinosaurs large, and scientists have obliged: many dinosaurs were not only large or even huge, but the largest were preposterously, outrageously, unreasonably big: the largest animals ever to walk on land. But the very large dinosaurs were not typical. Most dinosaurs did not exceed 30 feet in length, and the tail was bluff—it doubled the lengths of the animals without adding much to their weights. Most Cretaceous dinosaurs weighed more or less what large elephants do today. Among the findings of the 1970's is that most dinosaurs had babies, youngsters, and teenagers. Hardly surprising news, of course, but for years the evidence was overlooked in favor of the more dramatic "big stuff." Furthermore, we now know of remarkably small specimens. *Compsognathus,* a two footer, until very recently reigned as the smallest of the small; however, a very juvenile specimen of *Psittacosaurus* has been described as barely 9 inches long! *Mussaurus* ("mouse lizard"), a new prosauropod from Argentina, was barely larger. *Nanosaurus* and *Othnielia* both ranged down to 2 feet. Nests with 15 specimens of hatchling *Maiasaura* (a species of hadrosaur) three to 6 months old and 3 feet long, were uncovered in Montana in 1978.

The very large dinosaurs were undoubtedly slow-moving, although they may have covered wide distances with their long legs. Hadrosaurs and ceratopsians may have run at 30 mph, ornithomimids at ostrich-like 60 mph. Large or small, fast or slow, dinosaurs

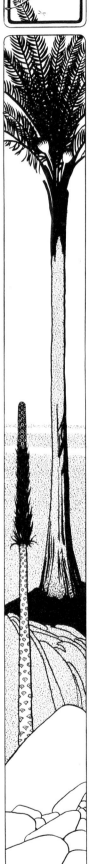

suffer from the reputation that they were stupid. Some indeed had rather small brains, but there has been exaggeration. More significantly, a few particularly small meat-eaters had enlarged brains that approached the size of brains found in birds of similar body size. *Tyrannosaurus rex* had one of the largest brains ever evolved in the history of life—a brain that was larger than more than 99% of mammals that ever lived, possibly as large as that of a chimpanzee or gorilla. Dinosaur brains were sufficient to permit considerable interesting behavior. Much evidence for male dominance behavior and female attraction behavior is preserved in bony display structures such as crests, frills, horns and spikes that have in the past been inadequately explained as defensive structures. Dinosaurs, like birds and lizards, may have made use of bright colors, rather than being confined to drab hues of black, white, brown and gray like most modern, color-blind mammals.

Remarkable new evidence from footprints, nests and mass death deposits raises the question as to whether or not some form of maternal care may have been practised.

Dinosaur Heresy—Dinosaur Renaissance

For the past decade, students of dinosaurs have chipped away at what the scientist Robert T. Bakker, a paleontologist at Johns Hopkins University, has termed "The Good Reptile" model of dinosaurs. This is the notion that to understand dinosaur biology we need only extrapolate from what we know about lizards or turtles or crocodiles. Today we know that they were bigger, faster, smarter, possibly more elaborate in their courtship and more caring of their young than their distant cousins.

Great effort was expended during the 1970's to unravel the thermal biology of dinosaurs. Living reptiles are *ectotherms* —they derive their body heat from an external source (the sun). They have low rates of metabolism and more or less sluggish levels of activity. Reptiles cool at night when the sun sets and warm during the day beneath the sun's rays; such variable body temperature is called *poikilothermy.* To call reptiles "cold-blooded" may be a misnomer, for a basking desert lizard may get very hot indeed!

Living birds and mammals are *endotherms*— they generate body heat internally.

They are active, have high rate of metabolism and their body temperatures remain constant day and night (homeothermy). Mammals and birds are generally warmer than reptiles at night, but may be cooler than certain reptiles by day.

The idea has been around for many years that dinosaurs, being more bird-like than crocodile-like in their anatomy, may have been bird-like in their physiology as well. Dinosaurs *look* like organisms built for high levels of activity—they simply don't look like slugs! Ten years ago, Robert T. Bakker presented a very forceful case for warm-bloodedness and endothermy in dinosaurs —*all* dinosaurs. He has since elaborated and defended the idea repeatedly, and the concept of active dinosaurs has gained much currency. During the same time period, John H. Ostrom of Yale University demonstrated that there exists a direct link between small meat-eating dinosaurs and birds. Upper Jurassic *Archaeopteryx* has for more than a century been regarded as the first bird; without its feathers, *Archaeopteryx* is a coelurosaur. The direct link between endothermic birds and meat-eaters, and the finding that meat-eaters had large brain size, encourage the view that flesh-eating dinosaurs may have been endothermic. Additionally, Robert T. Bakker has shown that the rarity of meat-eaters compared with the abundance of plant-eating dinosaurs found as fossil is exactly what one would expect *if* the meat-eaters were warm-blooded endotherms whose food requirements were very high. Others have found that even the microscopic structure of dinosaur bone resembles that of mammals and differs from that of living and fossil reptiles. The idea of endothermic dinosaurs is enormously appealing, and conditions a view of dinosaur biology that differs radically from that based on a strictly reptilian view of life. There is no longer any real controversy about whether dinosaurs were warm-blooded or not, in the sense that large dinosaurs, even with low rates of metabolism, would have had difficulty ridding themselves of excess heat. But large size seems to be a problem for endotherms, not an asset. The huge quantities of heat produced by active endotherms could have been lethal. Most paleontologists seem to believe that dinosaurs were special animals; that stereotypes provided by living reptiles on the one hand, and by birds and mammals on the other, fail to define the actual condition of dinosaurs. Because the stereotypes fail, dinosaurs must simply be considered in their own rights as wonderful, fascinating and sophisticated creatures—creatures that have not been duplicated.

Names

In dinosaur paleontology, names abound; some euphonious, some cacophonous, some felicitous, some rather unpronounceable. Four year old prodigies embarrass their elders by being able to rattle off 20 polysyllabic names. There is much more to paleontology than a name however, which by itself is static. Apart from the dramatic narrative in this book, we clearly establish a base of fact for most of the dinosaurs we discuss. Let us take as an example *Brontosaurus,* more properly known as *Apatosaurus:*

What are its relationships? It is a *sauropod,* the same suborder (group) to which *Alamosaurus, Haplocanthosaurus* and many other dinosaurs that we discuss belong. Furthermore, it belongs to the *Order Saurischia,* which means it had a lizard-like pelvis.

What were its eating habits? It was a herbivore. It ate flora. Cycads, ferns and broadleaf conifers were important parts of its diet, but we cannot guess how much of which.

What was its size? 60 to 80 feet. Some dinosaurs are known from both young and old specimens (that is, from both small and large individuals). Most specimens of *Apatosaurus* are of nearly adult size.

What was its weight? 10 to 30 tons. These are estimates, of course, but are probably reasonably accurate. Brontosaurus certainly weighed more than an elephant (4 to 6 tons), less than a blue whale (100 tons).

The height and weight statistics sited for a dinosaur refer to the range of known heights and weights of that dinosaur based on recorded fossil specimens. Where young animals are known, the weight range, like the size range, is correspondingly wider. If no more than one specimen of a dinosaur has been recorded, then no range is given.

Height and weight statistics for a dinosaur do not necessarily include the specifications for the specific illustrated dinosaur.

When did it live? It lived during the Upper Jurassic Period. This is very important, because collectively dinosaurs lived for 140 million years, but individual kinds lived only a few million years at most. No error is made more frequently in books and movies than to mix dinosaurs from different periods. For instance, *Coelophysis* lived *before Brontosaurus,* and *Tyrannosaurus rex* lived 75 million years *after Brontosaurus* was gone.

Where did it live and what were conditions like? Wyoming, Colorado and Utah; and flood plains, along river banks and lake shores, in rivers and lakes. Every animal has a limited geographic distribution as well as chronological one. Very few dinosaurs are found in widely separate parts of the world. In some cases we have a clear idea of what specific environments the fossil was found in; in other cases we know only in very general terms what conditions were like.

We have prepared this information for most of the dinosaurs we discuss. For each animal, it is found in a column adjacent to the text or illustration in which each animal plays a role.

Envoi

Dinosaurs simply will not go away. Their appeal is universal, an appeal to the imagination that is as natural as eating and breathing. A small minority of those who daydream as children do about a vanished world elect to carry on the tradition of the scientific study of dinosaurs. We search for solutions to mysteries and in so doing attract future generations of dreamers. Museum skeletons may seem austere; with this book we hope to flesh out the bones and fire the imaginations of those who would look to the past.

WELCOME TO THE MESOZOIC ERA

by William Service

Before we accept a welcome to the Mesozoic world, let us take one panoramic glance at our own, at the breadth and depth and extent of contemporary mammalian life—one glance, without commentary. Blue whale . . . shrew . . . giraffe . . . groundhog . . . bat . . . walrus . . . elephant . . . desert rat . . . mountain goat . . . mole . . . gazelle . . . lemur . . . .

The span of life called the Mesozoic began 235 million years ago and ended 63 million years ago. So thoroughly identified with the reign of the dinosaurs is the Mesozoic world that it is easy to slight the concurrent existence of fish, insects, lizards, crocodilians, turtles, the obscure founders of the mammalian line and later, birds.

We approach the Mesozoic through the hundred million years or so preceding it. In that span, when all the continents were jammed together, aberrant fish in the form of amphibians colonized the land. Although the lines surviving to our day—frogs and newts—tend to be small, damp, and soft, the amphibians of the time developed into many kinds of large heavy-boned animals who inhabited forests and flatlands as well as marshes. The most important of those animals were the reptiles, and in that assemblage were the therapsids, diverse creatures who seemed about to initiate the great mammalian sweep into the future. Hair, tooth formation, details of skull structure, articulation of ankle, set of jaw . . . the creatures with some or all of those mammalian characteristics abounded, some large and fierce, some large and vegetarian, some small and scurrying. However bizarre they may appear in our eyes, they were, in their development and in their exploration of their world,

"conservative": whether on dry land or in marshes or in trees, they tended to keep four feet on the ground—or whatever—and to stay out of the sky and deep water. As they were poised, nevertheless, to march across the continents into modern times, something happened, and this great assemblage was suddenly, over the course of thirty million years or less, squeezed down to a narrow file of animals running for the small niches available to them. Arboreal or burrow-dwelling, these ancestors of the mammals must have foraged mainly for invertebrate provender.

What befell the rest of the assemblage was the fatal success of a smallish sprawling crocodile like creature, a theocodont, who, over the eons managed to work its legs under its body and then to get most of its weight on its hind ones for bipedal movement: the forerunner and prototype of the dinosaur (one branch of which promptly and heavily reverted to a four-footed stance), the pterosaur, and, later, the bird. Before a third of the Mesozoic was past, this terrestial host had established several anatomical and behavioral styles: Carnivorous, all bipedal, ranging from small, light and swift to the truly huge; herbivorous, some on all fours, ranging from the small to the prodigious, and some bipedal, ranging from small to big. Many refinements and variations proliferated from those basic anatomical plans: horns, hooks, spikes, elongated necks and stumpy legs, dagger teeth, armored eyelids, clubs and helmets, elaborate senses and sprinter limbs.

"Archosaurs" . . . the name means ruling reptiles. To a human traveler in the world the archosaurs inherited, much of the terrain would appear superficially the same as today's. Marsh, seashore, coniferous forest, desert—it would require the eye of the botanist to tell the difference. What would be noted would be the absence of flowering forbs, bushes, and trees, and of grasses; and so, in landscapes where those would not predominate until late in the Mesozoic, the scene would present a feathery, spiky, frondy aspect, without the massive trunks and high-branched green shade of the hardwood forest. As the order, Archosaurs, radiated into families and genera and spread throughout that world, it left comparatively little developmental space for other orders of life. The largest of the archosaurs probably weighed only a little less than the blue whale—the largest creature known ever to have existed—and were certainly the largest animals to have walked on Earth. At the other extreme, an elegant little carnivore, less than two feet in total length, and a stumpy herbivore smaller than a pigeon, left, in effect, gaps only big enough for shrew-size creatures to inhabit. While most of the large herbivores could have looked down in multiples on today's giraffe, the Archosaur order did not develop diggers and burrowers such as our groundhog. Taking to the air, the order's unfeathered pterosaurs may have lacked the sophisticated aerial achievements of the bat, yet the wingspan of some of them dwarfed the condor's—indeed, some of the pterosaurs' remote Archosaur relatives initiated the entire avian succession. On the landscape of Earth, to the traveler in the world of the Mesozoic, the sight of an animal half again the size of an elephant, but an eater of flesh, is imposing enough. What gives longer pause, is that for every one of those adult monsters there had to have been many more of the same kind, cat-size, lynx-size, jaguar-size, tiger-size, lion-size, and on up . . . An acrobatic little dinosaur scampering along in the treetops—the idea seems incon-

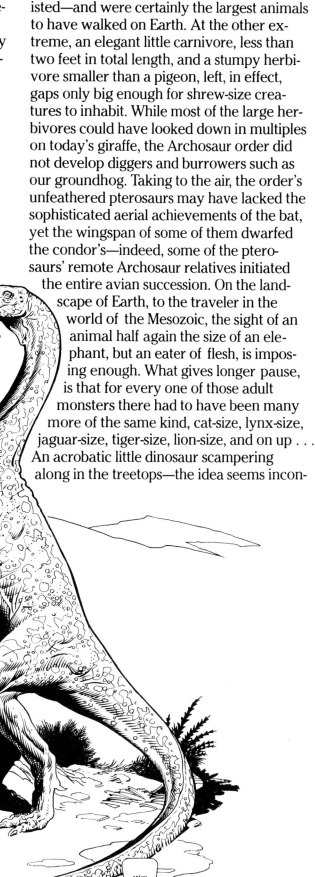

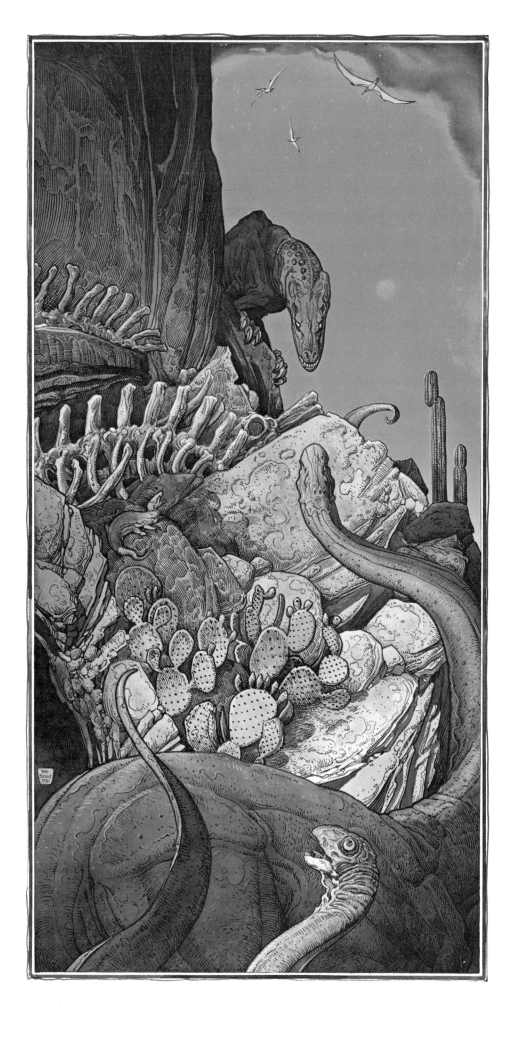

gruous, and indeed the remains of such an animal have never been found. Possibly our ancestors held that niche, possibly the capability to travel that way simply may not have existed in the dinosaur genes, or possibly the relative poverty of the Mesozoic domain—no seeds, fruits, or nuts until very late in the era—was the factor; in any case the dinosaurs' way of exploiting the tops of trees was to reach up and eat it all.

Deep desert, high alp, deep sea, snowy waste: all were left virtually unpopulated by the dinosaurs. Throughout the Mesozoic, however, there tended to prevail less of those extremes and a great deal more of the welcoming climes than prevail today. In herds and packs and one by one, the dinosaurs migrated throughout the choice lands, sometimes leaving the fossil footprints by which man could measure the walking speed of the animal in thick mud. From anatomical studies—shin to thigh ratios, relative weights, knee and hip articulation—the running speeds of various dinosaurs have been estimated and compared to the ostrich's, or gazelle's, or rhinoceros', depending on the species. Whatever their attainable velocities, the apparent high activity levels of many of the dinosaurs suggest the likelihood that they were endothermic, that perfectly or imperfectly their body temperatures remained near a high constant. Their activities, moreover, extended far beyond mere chasing or fleeing, grazing or flying. Some of them made nests, maintained them, extended a degree of parental care. They courted and dueled...

And some of them, toward the end, began to appear with large eyes to scan their world, larger brains to accommodate such vision and also to coordinate the movements of their agile limbs (and vice versa), and with highly rotatable forelegs by which their long-digited "hands" could be brought in apposition. The adaptations suggest something like today's little nocturnal tree-dweller, the tarsier, who, in addition, has an opposable thumb and a remote cousin, man.

The Mesozoic welcome to the dinosaurs was retracted about 63 million years ago and extended instead to the mammals. Was the demise of the dinosaurs a slow and orderly extinction or was it a sudden death? Did some violent celestial event, supernova or supermeteor, disrupt the benevolent interplay of earth's environment to set off a cas-

cading downfall of life forms, or did the wandering of the continents on their tectonic plates bring about a gradual inhospitality of climate to which they could not adapt? A complex array of evidence, conflicting but perhaps not finally indecipherable, continues to accumulate. Toward the end of the era, the number of different species declined in some regions of the earth. Other regions seemed to witness a proliferation of numbers and adaptive refinements. Over the crucial millennia, dinosaur eggs seem to have undergone an ominous thinning of shell thickness, perhaps a symptom of an order under heavy stress. Astronomers calculate the likelihood of a supernova and its effects on the biosphere. Geologists, seeking the impact zone of the great meteor, measure the presence of exotic minerals which might mark the site and extent of the impact precisely, and try to resolve the conflicting scenarios of doom which would ensue. Paleontologists survey the extent of life forms—among fish and shellfish, among trees and mosses, fliers, swimmers, scavengers—which indeed went down with the dinosaurs, to try to find the figure of the agent in the pattern of extinction. Others speculate on the importance of changing magnetic fields.

Whatever the agent, whether in a period of hundreds or many hundreds of thousands of years, the dinosaur reign collapsed with such ecological suddenness that upon their demise there were no grazing or browsing herbivores and no large carnivores; at the time, the largest animal on earth was probably a turtle, a crocodile, or a flightless bird and the largest mammal could have easily been eaten by the bird were it not that the latter was aquatic. In the rush to fill the vacuum of large animals, the first to arrive were other flightless birds, some of them imposingly massive. Stemming as they did from the dinosaur line, they possibly were prepared with a broader stock of potential genes for "large" size than were the long suppressed mammals . . .

We are going to look into the lives of the dinosaurs and of their kin, not their extinction. We go back into the Mesozoic, when our predecessors, some two hundred million generations (or even less) ago, lived in the fronds and rosettes of cycad trees or in burrows underneath, and ate bugs, worms, whatever came to hand.

THE TRIASSIC PERIOD

he Age of Reptiles—the Mesozoic Era—began about 230 million years ago. The first and shortest of the three periods of the Mesozoic was the Triassic Period, which lasted about 35 million years. The Triassic, like Gaul of old, was divisible into three parts in Germany, where it was first named.

The earth had a most unfamiliar appearance when the Triassic began. All of the continents were jammed together, forming a vast supercontinent known as Pangaea. Only a few tens of million years earlier, the south pole had skewered South Africa, and icey glaciers radiated outward, ravaging parts of present day India, Australia, South America and Antarctica—lands which were then nearest neighbors. By the Triassic, however, the thaw had well begun; indeed, in a number of places the period could be characterized as not only hot, but dry. This was a time when the land stood high and the seas were at one of their lowest extents during the 600 million years of conspicuous life on earth.

During the Triassic the land began to shudder as the continents first began to lumber

away from each other. Eastern North America began to pull away from North Africa (think of how the concave shoreline of our own continent complements the convex shape of northwest Africa). The scar of this activity consists of a series of long, narrow basins running from Nova Scotia to South Carolina, filled with rusty-colored shales, lavas and gray lake beds that give us a record of life at this time. A modern rift valley, showing continent-splitting underway, extends from South Africa to Israel. The proto-Atlantic Ocean and the Tethys Sea affected near separation of Laurasia (the firmly united continents of North America, Europe and Asia).

The southern continents of Africa, South America, Australia, Antarctica and India however, remained broadly joined and freely exchanged plants and animals among each other. This continent was called Gondwanaland.

Seas were widespread through the Cordilleran region of western North America, in the North American and European Arctic, and at times in Europe. Continental (dry land) rocks are known from eastern and

western North America, South America, Europe, South Africa, Antarctica, India, China and Australia.

Important plants of the Triassic included some groups that were common in the Late Paleozoic and were declining, and others that were on the ascent. Ferns and seed ferns of old were still much in evidence. Cycads were important, but not to the extent that they would become. Conifers of great variety were very important, including broad-leafed types such as ginkgos and narrow-leafed araucarians (today's Norfolk pine).

For vertebrates, the Triassic was a time of experimentation. Labyrinthodont amphibians of old had their last fling before extinction, so to speak, but some attained really impressive size before they went. The dominant reptiles were the therapsids, so-called mammal-like reptiles. In the Early Triassic of Gondwanaland, they were incredibly abundant, dog-like carnivores (such as the cynodonts) and bizarre, toothless, two-tusked dicynodonts that cropped the vegetation. Ironically, the closer the therapsids approached the mammalian condition as the period wore on, the smaller and the less

common they became. When true mammals appeared at the end of the Triassic, they were not only very small but very rare, and they remained so until the end of the Age of Reptiles. In this period appeared gliding lizards, turtles, frogs, a host of marine reptiles including icthyosaurs, plesiosaurs and strange, turtle-like placodonts. As therapsids declined, the archosaurs, the ruling reptiles, proliferated into a variety of types, most of which did not survive the Triassic. Included were large, sprawling proterosuchians; pseudosuchians showing various stages of four-legged or two-legged stance; heavily-armored aetosaurs; and large, crocodile-like phytosaurs with nostrils perched on the tops of their heads. Progressive groups that appeared towards the end of the Triassic were true crocodiles, pterosaurs, and best of all, dinosaurs.

Little coelurosaurs and lumbering prosauropods were the most characteristic dinosaurs of the Upper Triassic, and fabrosaurs and heterodontosaurs, though uncommon, were widespread. From these humble beginnings, dinosaurs rose to prominence for the rest of the Mesozoic.
—P.D.

THE JURASSIC PERIOD

The Jurassic Period ran from 195 million years ago to 140 million years ago. Its name comes from the Jura Mountains of France where rocks of that age were first recognized. The Jurassic was a time of warm, equable climates. Drought was a greater threat than frost, and in certain places at certain times, water was at least seasonally scarce. Seas transgressed on the land to a greater extent than they did in the Triassic Period.

The known Jurassic dinosaurs were overwhelmingly populous in two geographical areas—western United States (Late Jurassic Morrison Formation) and the Tendagura beds (of similar age), from Tanzania in eastern Africa.

Break-up of the continents was underway. North America and Europe remained resolutely sutured across Greenland, and this state of affairs persisted into the Age of Mammals. The North Atlantic continued to widen slowly, though it was still just a narrow slit. By the end of the Jurassic, South America had perceptibly inched away from Africa, and the South Atlantic had its origins as little more than an arm of the sea. Antarctica and Australia, conjoined, had set sail from the southern part of Africa, and India was adrift towards the north, though its impending collision with Asia, which would result in the Himalayas being thrown up, was still many years off.

The Tethys Sea was a major feature that traversed Europe and Asia for many millions of years; in fact, the Mediterranean Sea is a remnant of it. Eastern and central North America stood above the lapping waves during this time, whereas the Cordilleran region was under the sea. In the west, the first pulses of mountain-building began, the so-called Nevadan orogeny. Volcanoes erupted and granite was implaced in the Sierra Nevadas. Three or four separate times during this period, shallow seas reached down

from the Arctic Ocean as far south as New Mexico, then retreated. As the seas retreated for the last time back towards the north, a vast, rather thin sheet of sediment was laid down across a broad, low floodplain. The brightly colored mudstones—red, purple, green and gray, with occasional river-channel sandstones and lake limestones, are known as the Morrison Formation. In 1877, dinosaur remains were found there in abundance for the first time anywhere in the world. Dinosaurs were abundant in such Morrison Formation areas as Colorado, Wyoming, and Utah, and notable finds have been made in Montana, South Dakota, Arizona, New Mexico and Oklahoma as well. Ironically, far from showing abundant lakes and rivers and lush vegetation, these sediments seem to indicate a relatively harsh, seasonally dry climate that may have forced the dinosaurs to migrate in search of food.

For plants, the Jurassic was the age of cycads, which grew in a great variety of forms and sizes. Conifers, cone-bearing evergreens, were also important. Flowers were still lacking in the world at this time.

Dinosaurs, of course, dominated the land faunas. The tallest and longest of all dinosaurs were the sauropods. Although they had very large bodies, they were rather small-headed. As relatively unsophisticated herbivores, they held sway only during the Jurassic; although they did linger on in the Cretaceous period, they never again dominated. Another important herbivore in the period was the stegosaurus, a multi-plated dinosaur who did not survive the Jurassic. The ornithopods were small two-legged herbivores who bided their time until the Cretaceous. Large and small carnivores abounded during the Jurassic. Among non-dinosaurs, icthyosaurs, plesiosaurs, and marine crocodiles were conspicuous in the seas. Birds first appeared late in the period; mammals remained rare.   —P.D.

THE CRETACEOUS PERIOD

T he Cretaceous was the last of the three periods of the Mesozoic era. It lasted from 140 million to about 63 million years ago. The name *Cretaceous* comes from the Roman word for chalk; chalky marine deposits, filled with the shells of microscopic protozoans that teemed in the oceans of the Cretaceous, characterize the rocks from the period. It was a time of great flooding of the continents by the seas, rivaled only by the Ordovician seas some 350 million years earlier.

North America was divided in two by a shallow sea that ran from the Arctic Ocean to the Gulf of Mexico. Coastal sediments spilled off the land of the east coast from New Jersey to Georgia and along the Gulf Coast to Texas. During the latter half of the period, vigorous mountain formation was underway. This activity, known as the Laramide Orogeny, caused the rise of the ancestral Rocky Mountains, and sediments shed from the rising mountains were carried eastward and deposited by a series of short rivers into a vast delta stretching from Alberta to New Mexico, forming the western shore of the shallow continental sea. It was along this alluvial plain, perhaps two or three hun-

dred miles broad and fifteen hundred or more miles long, that dinosaurs roamed.

The Tetheys Sea persisted in Europe, and chalk, famous in England, can be found in Belgium, Holland and Denmark as well. In the Early Cretaceous Period, a vast swamp-lake-delta complex, referred to as the Weald, was installed in southern England and Belgium. Wealdan dinosaurs were among the very first to be discovered and described (*Iguanodon,* by Mantell, in 1825). In Saharan Africa, tropical swamps prevailed, and these too were populated by dinosaurs. Others existed in the regions that are now South America, India and Australia. One region of the earth that did not enjoy stong marine influence was Mongolia, where very important dinosaurs existed under rather dry, stressful conditions. Mongolian Cretaceous dinosaurs show strong similarities to those of western North America, and a land connection of some sort through Alaska and Siberia is indicated. Dinosaurs are also known to have existed in South America, India and Australia. By and large, the continents had attained their present positions by this time, though North America and Europe were still joined through Greenland, Europe and Africa separated by the Tethys Sea, and North and South America

were joined at most by a chain of islands (Central America was not yet in existence).

The Cretaceous started off warm enough, and fully tropical conditions were widespread. Coal swamps existed on the north slope of Alaska, and iguanodons wandered the Arctic island of Spitzbergen. A decidedly cooling trend began during the period, however, and by the end of the Cretaceous the climate had a distinct seasonality to it, although it was still warm temperate to subtropical. The cooling trend continued into the Age of Mammals, culminating in the Ice Age.

The outstanding biological characteristic of the Cretaceous was the modern aspect of the flora and fauna. The key was the appearance of flowering plants, the angiosperms. With their fast growth habit, and their efficient, fragrant and colorful reproductive systems, the flowering plants underwent an explosive adaptive radiation. Starting out as small weedy annuals, they rapidly exploited a wide variety of niches. As modern trees appeared, cycads and broad-leafed conifers diminished in number. A whole new fauna co-evolved with the flowering plants—pollinating insects and birds—and the animals that fed on them and on the plants they helped to propagate. Turtles, lizards, snakes, salamanders, and crocodilians all attained a modern aspect in this period, as did bony fishes in the sea. Modern mammals appeared, though they remained small. Possum-like marsupials were common first, and at the very end of the period insect-eating placental mammals became populous, the ancestors of the great host of familiar mammals of today. Plesiosaurs and ichthyosaurs still plied the seas, but the latter in particular suffered when a new group of marine reptiles arose and flourished: The mosasaurs were a group of lizards that went to sea and attained large skulls, ferocious teeth, and grew to lengths of thirty feet. Pterosaurs still flew, but they were never common, and by the end they were eclipsed in number by birds of many kinds.

Far from being superannuated by such a novel world, the dinosaurs flourished with greater diversity and sophistication than ever before. Ornate duck-bills and horned dinosaurs attained a peak of tooth complexity that few mammals have ever rivaled. Large and small carnivorous dinosaurs abounded. The ankylosaurs, wide-bodied and heavily armored, and the still-lingering sauropods, lumbered like giants across the changing earth. —P.D.

THE DINO

CONTENTS

COMMUNITY

DAILY LIFE

DANGER

MOVEMENT

THE DINOSAUR BODY

SAURS

THE BABY

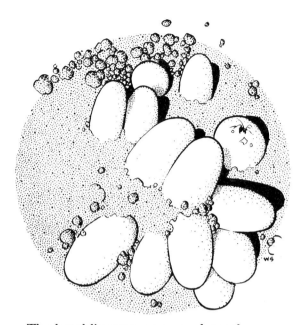

As big as or bigger than most other animals which hatch from an egg, this sauropod working his way clear of a shell emerges as the smallest baby, relative to its mother's size, who ever walked on land: a big hatchling, and yet a uniquely tiny baby. For in the deep footprint of a parent, this baby male and several siblings could easily curl up together. Even when he becomes steady on his feet and vigorous, he will not likely walk the distance from the outstretched head all the way to the tail of an adult in one continuous walk. It is just too far. A mother, browsing the tops of cycads and pulling up ferns and giant moss, eats in a day many times the body weight of her offspring. After the baby doubles and redoubles his own weight, and doubles that again and again, he will still be able to curl up in the parental footprint. Although he will grow too big for it after a while, several more doublings still will not prevent the young sauropod from strolling under the belly of a standing adult.

The image of the adult sauropod is prodigious; the shadow cast is almost endless. And yet this baby is *small.* How is he to survive long enough to match those dimensions? His teeth and claws are not dangerous and never will be. He has no special defensive equipment. At all stages of his growth, any predator who wants to catch him can do so in a few strides. But there is strength in numbers: the baby travels well-protected at the center of the sauropod herd. His line, despite its shortcomings, extends some 120 million years....

Camarasaurus
sauropod
saurischian
herbivore
15-65 ft.
1-25 tons
Upper Jurassic
Western U.S.:
lake complex

The hatchling moves away from the clutch of eggs. From above, almost out of sight, at the end of a neck twice as long as the body, his parent's head swings down and around to touch her nose to the baby. The adult head is not many times larger than the offspring, and so the two animals briefly are seen to belong to the same line. Only so close can the parent recognize the small one. The baby does not recognize the parent, but does not try to flee. He and the rest of the brood, small, gently lumbering, take advantage of the last protection the adults can give them for the next several seasons: they follow the swath of trampled vegetation which stretches, cleared of raptors, down to the marsh. There, of the many, some few will survive, grow, and eventually fill a parental footprint with one massive foot of their own.

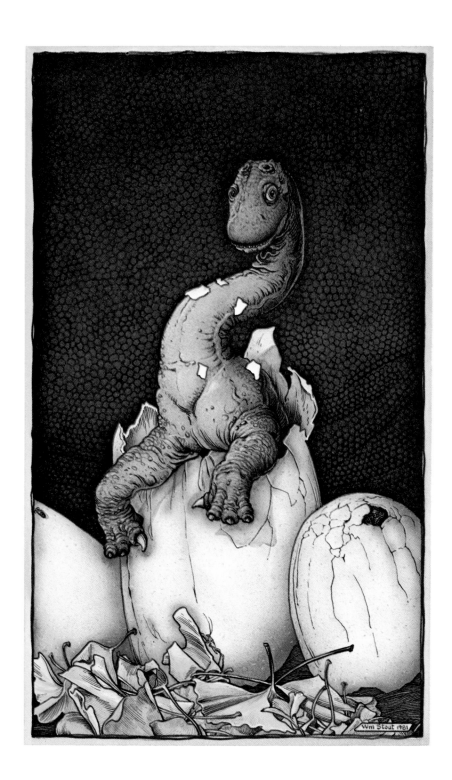

CHILDHOOD

U nder attack, young ankylosaur lashes out. The three-knobbed club at the end of his tail, a thing more massive than his head, strikes flush on the side of his adversary's neck. Vexed, she hits back with her own clubbed tail, then retreats a few steps in order to drive her longer shoulder spikes in past the defense of his haunch spikes. He tries to work the array of horns around his head into the softer hide of her underbelly. She wriggles clear. . . .

What the two are disputing is claim to a clump of milkweed-like plants: they thrive on vegetation which most other herbivores find unpalatable or even poisonous. One exception is the young sauropod now approaching, who can digest the buds and new growth at the top of the plants, but which, stretch as he will, and tilt up on hind legs as he will, he cannot reach. The ankylosaurs, taking in the situation, hiss furiously at him and make a short charge. Young sauropod keeps on eating. They pull up broadside to him, rapping him smartly all over his body with blows which in later years could break the shin of a tyrannosaur or cave in its frag-

ile skull. Young sauropod tries to evade the hits and eat at the same time, and finally trundles off.

It is a critical phase for the sauropod, one to grow out of quickly. He had fed his growth by glutting himself on the soft browse of algae and water plants, but then quit the marshes along with the rest of his ravenous generation when he could no longer harvest enough to keep himself fed.

The transition to land is difficult, dangerous—he is still too small to hide inside the mighty circling wall of a herd. A new kind of hunger sets young sauropod's short neck craning about until he sees what he is instinctively hungering for: fine sharp gravel for his gizzard, which will aid him in digesting his food. Hearing something as he swallows, young sauropod does not flee, but approaches: the sounds of browsing attract a browser. The fresh tender bracken he finds is good forage, but the truculent young torosaur who is grazing upon it does not intend to share. The impact of torosaur's horns—used not so long ago to break out of his egg—is not hard enough to break through sauropod's hide. Still lacking the tree-cutting bite of his elders, torosaur depends upon the ferns, and so he guards them by rushing at the competition. Young sauropod shoves ahead. Then suddenly, at a rustle, a scrape of claw on rock alien to them both, they halt. These two herbivores, separated in time as well as in distance from the protection of their respective herds, anticipate the origin of that sound and then see it: Stalking nearer, a young tyrannosaur snaps up a lizard slow enough to catch, an insect big enough for her to bother with. Tyrannosaur is lean to emaciation, and small, very small, but both herbivores automatically watch her every move with the highest alertness until she has passed on by. . . .

It is a critical phase of life for every member of the younger generation.

Opposite:

Allosaurus
carnosaur
saurischian
carnivore,
scavenger

Brontosaurus
(Apatosaurus)
sauropod
saurischian
herbivore

Below:

Tarchia
ankylosaur
ornithischian
herbivore
12 ft.
1500 lbs.
(adult size)
Upper Cretaceous
Mongolia:
arid semi-desert

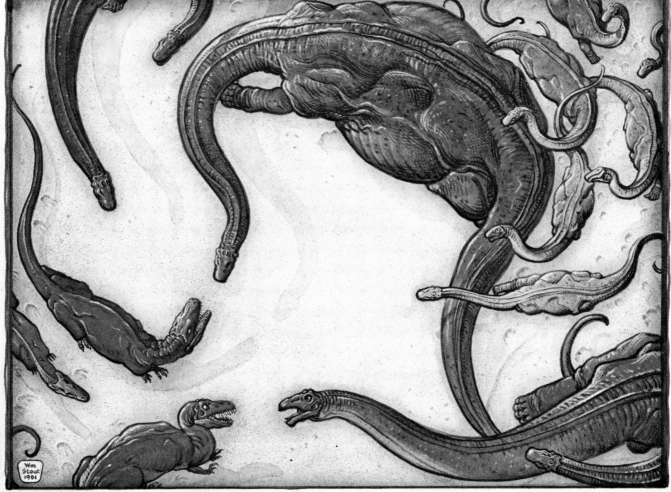

BROTHERS AND SISTERS

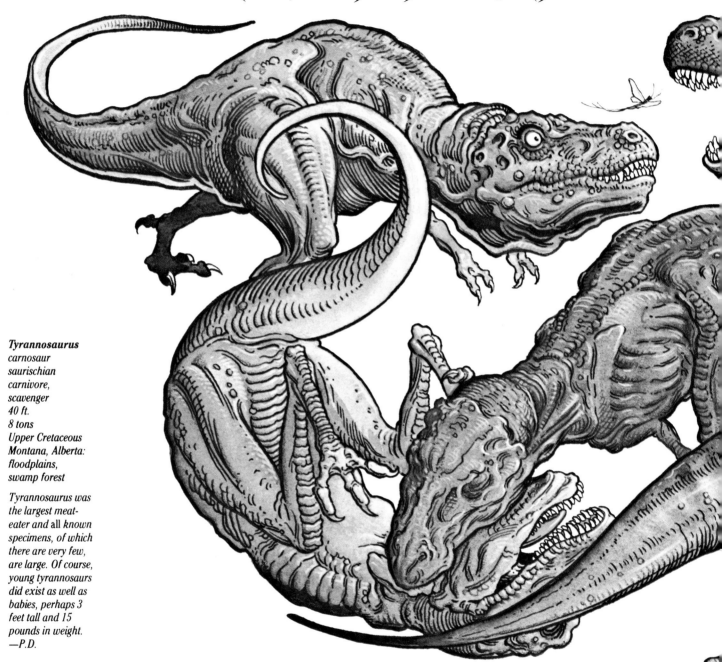

Tyrannosaurus
carnosaur
saurischian
carnivore,
scavenger
40 ft.
8 tons
Upper Cretaceous
Montana, Alberta:
floodplains,
swamp forest

*Tyrannosaurus was
the largest meat-
eater and all known
specimens, of which
there are very few,
are large. Of course,
young tyrannosaurs
did exist as well as
babies, perhaps 3
feet tall and 15
pounds in weight.
—P.D.*

T he tyrannosaurs enjoy their rank in the animal world. The giants among them move in a stately tread from carcass to carcass to dine and occasion- ally take part in a kill. They mate with a heavy stumbling grapple and clamp of tails, pelvises, and hind limbs, and leave great clutches of eggs. Few of the hatchlings survive their first season, but

once of sufficient stature, their pack's very simple hunting and protective maneuvers are enough to guarantee easy survival. The juveniles chase each other, wrestle with deadly talons carefully interlocked, trip and shoulder each other to the ground, administer practice death bites. Impressing themselves upon each other, they form the bond which will lead to success in mating and pack behavior.

THE HERD

A herd of the great sauropods plunges into the mature forest to browse. The larger brontosaurs strip the leaves, nuts, and fruit from thirty-five feet or more up, and on down to the ground. Some trees above their reach yield to the push of fifty tons or more of dinosaur, whereupon the younger members of the herd share the provender.

The limitations of sauropod feeding apparatus—small mouths and teeth, light jawbones, narrow gullets—suggest a diet of succulent vegetation, while their body size necessitates a great deal of it. And so they have to keep moving. They leave behind not a wrecked forest but a changed one: the largest trees standing, now above a well-manured earth open to the sun or thickly mulched under bark and trampled branches; a myriad long-suppressed seeds, sprouts, and saplings about to begin their race for the light. That tangled green proliferation will feed a new migration of thriftier herbivores, among which will be a number of creatures small enough to appreciate occasional beetles

and worms in their fare: hatchling sauropods.

Browsing steadily, from riverbanks and shallows as abundantly as from treetops, the herd converts a prodigious mass of vegetation into two products, dinosaur and fertilizer. Moving on, it transports a wealth of both products from one range to the next, and the ranges may span a continent. Arriving at an old breeding ground, the herd may be joined by young sauropods now large enough to begin the new way of life.

The death of an adult, by old age or predator attack, is an event of great local import. A hill of flesh and bone on the ground, thirty, fifty, eighty tons of it: an entire community will gather, and multiply, and remove it. Thus the migration of the ponderous animal does not stop after death, but changes direction from linear to radial. From the terrific allosaur through a host of lesser predators, to rove beetles and maggots, and finally down to fungi and bacteria—all disperse the dead sauropod's substance throughout the region and give new richness to a soil from which will grow lusher, greener trees, possibly for a return visit of the herd.

Brontosaurus (Apatosaurus)
sauropod
saurischian
herbivore
60-80 ft.
10-30 tons
Upper Jurassic
Wyoming,
Colorado, Utah:
floodplains,
shorelines, lakes,
rivers (i.e., in water
and on dry land)

HOME

The first megalosaur sprang up, bellowed, came at them. The herd of iguanodons did not panic but wheeled toward the high-banked river. The second hunter broke from cover too early, giving the herd time to turn and stride heavily away along the bank. The two predators, the only sort large enough to attack the herd, were as slow as their prey: the chase lumbered along, with one great three-toed foot squashing the print of the one preceding. One megalosaur was now directly behind the herd while the other paced along on the flank. The land dipped to where a meander of water joined the river. The pursuit slowed to a ponderous plod across the stretch of soft silty ground now churned to muck. Slogging through bog too soft to hold a print, the iguanodons heaved themselves forward, dug their front feet into hummocks, pulled, shoved off. The two megalosaurs, lurching clumsily, fell behind but persisted as the footing gradually became firmer.

A small troop of light-bodied coelurosaurs gathered. The squash and suck of mud under the struggling animals and the saccadic rush of breathing seemed to presage a kill they might get in on. They swept in to frolic among the iguanodons: they harried their shanks, and sprang high to snap at necks and faces. If the coelurosaurs could turn the herd, or scatter it, or break its pace, they would have only to wait and watch until they ate. The iguanodons did not break stride as they lashed out the wicked spikes on their front feet, and moved closer to one another to crowd the movements of their harassers. Most of the coelurosaurs scrambled nimbly to the outside with nothing more than some rakes and gashes, but one of them got hit hard, got hit again by the next iguanodon, and fell. The foot which pressed him down gave an extra squeeze of talons in passing. The bleeding coelurosaur was still trying to get up when one of the megalosaurs arrived.

The megalosaur on the distant flank of the herd saw the body being shaken in the jaws of the other and pivoted in that direction, then was put off by the obvious meagerness of the prey and swung back toward the herd. Moving steadily along, the iguanodons followed a bend in the river which put the megalosaurs hopelessly behind them—a distance which one of the dispersing coelurosaurs traversed in a few breaths.

The members of the herd crouched and panted briefly, then set about cramming into their maws as much forage as rapidly as they could. Long tongues twined around bunches of leaves: a brusque jerk of the head was followed by noisy munching. In their wake, the vegetation stood stripped and shredded.

Toward the end of the day the herd broke up, with only the unmated males and females remaining together. The sun setting on this lean ragged landscape cast in high relief thick copses of intact vegetation, widely scattered billows of green-gold and orange throwing long shadows. One by one the iguanodons headed for these preserves. One large male, cheeks bulging, rotund with fresh forage, skirted such a bower, but not widely enough. A young male, large for his size, sounding out furiously, burst out of the undergrowth and charged him. The small one came to a stop just before contact. With jabbing spikes lacerating the air, he threatened to eviscerate the larger, who returned the threat, then moved on. He strode heavily across the cropped land until he arrived at the margin of another preserve. He stopped, uttered low staccato grunts and was answered. Only then did he begin to shove through the underbrush: a silence might have meant a killed mate, a waiting carnosaur. Entering a clearing in the middle of the bower, he was set upon by six or seven miniatures of himself and of the female walking behind them. The young grappled his shins, bestrode his tail and savaged it with their small sharp spikes. He swept them away, and with the backs or unarmed edges of front feet kept knocking them down and tumbling them until they quit. Then, on all fours, he ejected the fine-milled contents of his cheeks onto the ground. A mild convulsion emptied his stomach of the last browse of the day. The young, well-able to forage for themselves, nevertheless gobbled up this extra—leaves too high, twigs too tough—which would speed their growth through the most vulnerable period. While the young ate,

male and female shouldered each other, nuzzled . . . a remnant of their mating sequence. All then browsed until nightfall. when they huddled in warmth, silence, and some safety.

At sunup, the female would be the one to leave and forage with the herd. The male in turn would lead the young around and around the periphery of the clearing, ever enlarging his circle as he broke branches and bent small trees for them. Days later, when the bower had been entirely stripped from the inside out, they all would scatter to join one herd or another for seasons of continual movement until again mating pairs began to lag, stay behind, establish bowers.

Iguanodon
ornithopod
ornithischian
herbivore
15-30 ft.
1-6 tons
Lower Cretaceous
England, Belgium:
swamps beside large
lake complex

BREAKFAST AT DAYBREAK

W hen there was enough light to pick out the dark bare trunks of the magnolia grove, the ceratopsian came slowly awake. Massively fit, in the prime years of his life, nevertheless he struggled to his feet like one sick or wounded. Still percolating through his system were juices from yesterday's forage, when he had strayed from the herd to feed in a deadfall of cycad trees. In his mouth the texture of the moldering fronds lingered, on his tongue the strange taste of the foamy sap in the crowns . . . . He was now in an open wood already stripped bare by hadrosaurs, to a level as high as they could stretch. The ceratopsian accomplished a few ponderous steps and cropped savagely at a weed too bitter for even hadrosaur tastes.

Keeping apart from the rest of the herd, he chose a young magnolia to bring to earth. He wrenched it in the angles between his horns until its stiff, leathery leaves clattered together. The effort brought the bitter weed back up in his throat. Trying to walk the tree down, he could not even rattle the leaves. He ambled away to drink deeply from the pool of a running spring. Light from the risen sun struck obliquely through the sheared woods. Flies began to swarm around the already beetle-ridden dung of the hadrosaurs, and a few elegant dragonflies took off from the rushes around the pool to wing through the ground mists and pick them out of the air. The ceratopsian raised his dripping muzzle from the water and saw the willow tree on the opposite bank. Grunting in anticipation, he splashed across the pool to engage it.

He fixed his horns on either side of the trunk, then worked them up and down to tear the bark from it. With dainty precision the great blades of his beak peeled and cut strip after strip to be chewed and swallowed.

He licked dry the cool, tart wood. Then he clamped the trunk in his beak as high as he could, crushed it, and twisted the tree down. Starting with the leaves and long supple twigs, he went on to eat most of the willow, leaving only some chunks of macerated wood toward the base.

Another long drink, a long acrid stream of urine out: he was feeling stronger. As he tramped the forest floor, a few lithe opportunists skipped along to snap up whatever had to jump or scurry out of his way. Nearing an open sweep of plain, the ceratopsian saw a form not very different from the form of the slender creatures in his company, but enormously enlarged: Tyrannosaurus. The ceratopsian advanced as far as he could in the protection of the big trees. Halting at the last row, he lowered his head to raise up his vast escutcheon in the other's direction, then gave out a snort like the sound of a thick oak being split instantly crown to root. It was a sound, with modulations, which might alert his herd to danger, fire a rival's fury, warm and loosen the joints of a female, or warn off a predator.

It caught the tyrannosaur on the side of the head, stopped it. The carnosaur pivoted slowly to confront the ceratopsian, as for eons their ancestors had done, ancestors who had been changing for eons according to each other's evolving form and behavior. The ceratopsian would not challenge the carnosaur on the open plain, and the tyrannosaur knew better than to maneuver his unwieldy bulk through the woodland against so compact, well-armed and truculent an adversary. Thus poised, the two were at a standoff. Cautiously, the ceratopsian backed into the woods and left to rejoin his herd.

They were already at breakfast, smashing down whatever trees were not stout enough to stand before the charge. Occasionally a thwarted animal, head awry, would take a trunk in its beak and work left and right until the thing was girdled deeply enough to yield. So treated, a magnolia toppled and swatted earth near the returning male. He poached, nipping up the seed-studded dry fruit, then stripping the thick stiff leaves. His cohort joined him without protest. When the tree was bare and trampled, they moved on. And when finally the herd moved on, only scattered giants remained standing above the fertile rubble.

Styracosaurus
ceratopsian
ornithischian
herbivore
10-20 ft.
1-3 tons
Upper Cretaceous
Alberta:
lowland forest,
swamp, floodplain

THE SONGS

The breeding grounds are thronged with all manner of duckbills, all sizes and shapes. Where the territories of different types overlap, the variety of calls fill the air too full of sound to contain one more bray, honk, or trumpet. The small empty space they leave at the top of the register is crowded with the whistles and trills of birds.

A small-crested hadrosaur, his chest at first vibrating with richness of tone, gradually squeezes his call up his throat, through his crest, and out through his bill as a strident squawk. He calls again, this time chopping the sound into short bursts. With intimidating vocal display, each male celebrates his kind, his strength, and his ready virility, and how many leaves there are on however many mulberry trees he can enforce claim to. Some days, the females merely register their presence and, by timing their muted answers, communicate to the males that their mighty outcry is not being lost in empty air. The intensity of all this clamor has a disorienting, even dismaying effect on other animals. The great predators head one way, go another, drift away from the area.

Richer, deeper, thicker than any other animal tone heard in the air before or since is the bass call of the great-crested hadrosaur. From the mighty syrinx deep in his chest, the tone thunders in the longest sound-pipe in nature, emerging as a great shudder of air. The call is close to the harmonic sounds of earthquake, tornado, volcano . . . and instills almost the same fear among hadrosaur's enemies, who hear it in their ribs and throats and bones of the skull even more strongly than in their ears.

A young parasaurolophus in his first rut, braying with all his might, still cannot establish his space. He invades the area of an older male, collides with him, shoulders and shoves with a force and enthusiasm matched by the older male. With their duck-like beaks, they inflict irritating bites on each other. Forefeet to the ground, they exchange swinging thumps of the tail to head and neck. They persist until the younger,

exhausted, moves off. The older, in a mix of sexual heat and an urge to bully the other out of any part in the mating season, strides after and tries to mount him. The younger breaks clear and they go through much the same sequence of shoving and buffeting as before. The younger again retreats. His tired rival, however, lacks the zeal to drive him completely from the arena, and so the young male is able to claim just enough land for possible courtship.

The slow-moving air brings tangled streamers of scent for all the different clans of hadrosaurs to sort through. The tread of the hadrosaurs is stately. Their frenetic vocalizing, a vibrant motley of tones and pitches and phrases, more accurately indicates the state of things.

A female, walking and grazing, moves into the range of the young male: she is a speck in the distance to his eyes; to his exquisitely sensitive nose, she is a pervasive, intoxicating presence. He calls her to him. Moving through a copse toward the open ground he controls, she appears, disappears, reappears, and then, in full sight of him, awash in the stream of his excited outcries, she meanders in the direction of his rival's territory. Both males stride toward her, the younger firing out nasty whickerings, the older beaming the final phases of the mating song. Attracted to the young male's long and colorful crest, the female attends his angry noise, and stops. The young male's thorax swells, there is a pause, then he crushes the air out in the one great, deep tone. It ends. When his chest again swells, hers does also. Her song rumbles out not quite so deeply as his. The pulse of their dark dissonance throbs in the air like a heartbeat. The bond is formed.

Moving off together, they rub the lengths of their necks together, nuzzle each other everywhere, turn and twine necks to the extent their thickness allows. She licks flecks of algae from the young male's mouth. They separate. He gives out a soft purring shadow of the deep tone. A slow, uncurling sweep of her tail is his reward. She honks. Scent, sound, sight, all signal her exact readiness. He runs at her, clasps on with forelegs,

shoves with a hindleg to lever her tail out of the way in order to join and thrust into her. She pivots fluidly away from the shove to turn out from under him and butt him on the base of the neck. With the little hooves of her front feet dug into earth, she buffets her haunches into his, then cavorts away. The inexperienced young male, his sequence broken, simply stands there, then aimlessly scratches and grooms, then actually grazes for a few moments until the unfocused surge of excitement blocks all movement and threatens to break out in a frenzy of biting and kicking. The female, not inexperienced, cautiously approaches. She rubs the length of her neck along his. She licks flecks of algae from the young male's mouth. He purrs a shadow of the deep tone.

Parasaurolophus
hadrosaur
ornithischian
herbivore
20-30 ft.
2-3 tons
Upper Cretaceous
Alberta:
floodplains, lakes, rivers, swamps (i.e., in and out of water)

NESTING

S ensing the wind, scanning the crests of the low hills, listening for the good and the bad footfalls, the hadrosaurs bray and trumpet their perceptions to one another. They flare the bright tissue between crest and nape of neck: the displays of color which in breeding time may have signaled instant heat or a challenge to combat, now signal danger, safety, doubt through subtle differences in hue which only a hadrosaur can detect. They are tending their young at the nesting site.

Between hatching and shin-high, the young are helpless—one easy bite for a predator. The adults, becoming more gaunt with each day, drive to good browsing the small, drag in boughs and saplings for the

Saurolophus
hadrosaur
ornithischian
herbivore
25-40 ft.
3-6 tons
Upper Cretaceous
Alberta, Mongolia:
floodplain, swamp
forest, river, lake

smaller, and chew up fodder to heap in front of the smallest. With soft kicks, harmless bites, and inconsequent chases, the adults train their young. In the great hurry to get safely through this vulnerable stage, some of the hatchlings, too slow afoot or too slow in growing, are crushed underfoot. Neither sibling nor adult notices, except to avoid touching the body. Should an attack of carnosaurs prevail, the herd will retreat, leaving for them the hindmost. Yet the rough nurturance works. Among the few dozen of the several broods, a hatchling with a shriveled stump of a front leg does not starve, is not trampled, is not seized up in the great jaws of a predator. He romps with serious intent, studies the patterns of his world, races along an awkward three-legged diagonal by which he keeps up. His cohort sprawls through the marsh: he propels himself like a crocodilian. Adults, bending saplings for the young, may hold them down longer for him than for the others, or they may not. He works his one arm as the others use their two. The nesting season done, it is time for the herd to disperse, one member just barely in sight or sound of the next. The cripple, like any other, strikes out toward the far pasture.

LUNCH

n the morning of their lives, she and her kind dabbled like ducks for soft swamp vegetation and for the aquatic life swarming in it. In the company of six . . . seven . . . eight others, she had been venturing inland for the more substantial browse her growing body required. Gentle, wary creatures, these hadrosaurs would first swim their mighty way invariably to the windward shore, their exuberant wakes rolling in after them. Pausing to dip for brunch, they would monitor the wind which blew from land to water. Equipped with the most sensitive and elaborate of olfactory systems, they would patrol the shore until every predator was located, identified, and its movements accounted for. Only then would the hadrosaurs gather to browse as far as they dared in the corridor of safe air. As they moved peacefully along in an uneven line, the first to detect a blood scent or any suspicious movement would bleat an alarm to send them all trundling back into

Brachylophosaurus
hadrosaur
ornithischian
herbivore
20-30 ft.
3-4 tons
Upper Cretaceous
Alberta:
rivers, swamps,
floodplains

the water. Occasionally, but not often, their compact phalanx would tumble an incompetent or undersized carnosaur out of action. If not, if one of their group never made it back to the lake, still they could absorb the loss. The hadrosaurs were thriving.

Now, in the noon of her life, the young female has to forage too far inland to allow a return to the lake by evening. She clambers up the lake shore. A shining coat of water flows down her body and limbs into puddles. Her kind move inland together, scything through sedge and bracken, heads swinging slowly left and right on long necks. To the clipping and snipping is added a peculiar milling sound: she lifts her head high and runs the contents of her packed cheeks through multifile teeth until what she swallows is purée. She resumes grazing only after seeing another of the herd stand erect. While the others eat, at least one among them stays upright, milling forage and scanning the wind and terrain. Keen not only of nose but also of eye and ear, the hadrosaurs' inland strategy is simply to detect the predator before it can detect them.

The female's harvesting appears utterly tranquil at first, but in the way she snatches at the undergrowth she reveals something between eagerness and anxiety. Bracken, sedge, whatever, the meal is not sufficient. The range is overgrazed and the sun is hot. Overlooked in her friends' grooming, the last few leeches on her flanks shrivel, drop off.

They all want the lake, but in hunger press on and achieve for the first time the low rain-catching hills. It is only here that lunch can truly commence. She, like the others, jostles as much for the contact as in competition, stretching high for acorns, pine nuts, and mulberry leaves. They burble and snort for no reason except to circulate appreciation among themselves. A shaded forb spreads enormous succulent leaves near her feet. She stoops to gather them, the sheaf folding fanwise to go into her mouth.

Not far off, another herd, even more bizarrely crested, also browses. Just beyond them, a smaller type, thescelosaur, noisily grazes the palmetto. Herds of these and other hadrosaurs dot the landscape to the horizon. Among them, uncountable egg-laden females await nightfall to restock the lakes, marshes, and estuaries which earlier in the year were a muddy turmoil of hatchlings. In their multiplicity, in their range, in their sheer numbers, surely they represented the dinosaur wave of the future, until the future collapsed.

Parasaurolophus
hadrosaur
ornithischian
herbivore
20-30 ft.
2-3 tons
Upper Cretaceous
Alberta:
floodplains, lakes,
rivers, swamps (i.e.
in and out of water)

THE DUEL

1980
Wm
Stout

T he herd assails the world with a collective smash to the neck or body: the impact, on a competing herbivore or attacking predator, is so great that a dome of bone four to nine inches thick is required to protect the pachycephalosaur's head. The males define themselves to each other by ramming domed skull against domed skull. Thoughout the herd, which is tightly knit though widely dispersed in its upland range, any meeting becomes an occasion for sniffing, shoving, and a few light knocks to head and flanks. The smallest clamber up rocks to butt each other off, for training and exercise and sport.

When the herd begins to assemble for the mating season, a complicated and incessant bickering agitates the females. Never brought to formal resolution, their head-knocking is limited to three collisions at most, and many of these are perfunctory swipes delivered in passing. Although no female seems to go out of her way to confront another, by the end of a day each one will in all likelihood have exchanged at least one brisk nod-and-buck with every other.

The spring heat intensifies. Of the males, the adults carefully stay aloof from each other. They court the females heavily, rubbing necks, flaunting, engaging in mock copulations which the unready females deny with a simple tuck of the heavy tail or repulse with a gentle butt on the male's

neck. The juveniles, aroused by the activity, the loaded atmosphere, batter each other intermittently all day long.

Invading the highland meadow, the herd segregates by sex. Male threatens male with posturing, bleats, feints, bluffs. The females save their combative energies for predators and competing herbivores. They will eat as much as they can, then mate, then eat again to stock up before retreating to the hills and crags.

The herd's hold on the rich meadow is a temporary triumph of busy aggression. Although strong and maneuverable in rugged country, the pachycephalosaurs lack the speed of the plains dwellers, and once engaged by a predator, an individual is helpless.

But now, able to stay together in communal defense, they own all the world they need.

A younger male prances, rears to challenge an older male, who answers the gesture, and both drive forefeet down into the ground. In unison they rear again, then plunge to a four-legged stance from which they spring at each other. That first bone-deep crunch raises the head each of the females who resume grazing before the sound of the second. The males crack heads as if in the middle of their domed skulls was a common ache which only hard hitting could cure. They bounce off each other, pass head to haunch and, grunting furiously, pivot around and around each other trying for a winning angle . . . .

Pachycephalosaurus
ornithopod
ornithischian
herbivore
14-18 ft.
500-1000 lbs.
Upper Cretaceous
Montana:
floodplain,
swamp forest

Having watched the first hits, the other males quickly set to pounding each other: the joust becomes a brawl. Just as the leading male wins his advantage and pummels the ribs of the challenger, the two smallest males leave off their own fight to ram into the side of the leader. He balances groggily on all fours, is given one great blow to the pate by his first challenger, and lowers himself slowly to the ground. The challenger immediately starts in on one of the two who rescued him.

The females show no interest in the tangle of winning and losing; they merely look up now and then to make sure the fray is still going on. Sometimes a male beaten into submission rises to defeat a conqueror now wobbly from further combat, and sometimes not. But finally the tumult winds down,

leaving four males crouching in defeat and three still standing, but with all the fight battered out of them. One of the three becomes victor through a mild rearing challenge which the other two do not answer. The fight is over. The females now mill around, and attend.

More or less in the order of win and lose, the males, not an unbloodied pate among them, stride or waddle from the arena. They make their way toward the cluster of females, the victor, in the lead, preparing to assert his right to take the choicest females who present themselves to him. Which females will present themselves to him, as well as the mating order for all the others, the pachycephalosaur females, through a season's complicated and incessant bickering, have already determined.

THE HOIST

At a distance from the rest of the herd, the two triceratops go at each other head-on. The great bony shields which cover the head and back of the neck protect the triceratops against fatal thrusts, but not against bloody gouging, pain, exhaustion, or overheating; and it is usually the accumulation of those factors which decides the outcome of the duel. The older of the two is in some way aware of this and is content to back off and charge, back off and charge. His six prongs engage, twist against the younger's set, rake flesh. Each triceratops streams blood from many shallow gashes. As the number of collisions increases, the older realizes that his opponent is not becoming discouraged, or weaker, or even more fatigued. Their horns interlock again: the older violently twists right, twists left. His rival will have none of it.

They back off, balanced masses in nearly exact symmetry, but this time two slight differences occur which, in his inexperience, the younger triceratops perceives as signs of weakness: First, the older does not go back the entire distance necessary for a full speed charge, thus compelling the younger to do likewise or be struck while moving back. Next, the older drops his head lower than before, so low that his pronged beak whispers through the trampled sedge.

The two pairs of long brow-horns have just cracked together when the older's intention is made clear: colliding at less than full speed, he has time to slip his single prong precisely under the apex of the younger's jaw. He hoists. Action stops, then the younger triceratops arches furiously to work himself up and off it. He finds himself still staring up at the sky. The older drives upward just a little harder, giving enough of the auger to make his point: any further resistance will drive the prong through the floor of his rival's mouth and next will ensue a sundered jawbone. The younger signals surrender out of his nostrils, a wheezing sigh which seems to go on forever.

Torosaurus
ceratopsian
ornithischian
herbivore
25 ft.
5 tons
Upper Cretaceous
Wyoming:
floodplain

THE POOL

Under the coat of dust, the male's mating colors were still bright, but he no longer flaunted them. The female's pattern of leaf green, black, and olive stood out bold and rich against the dark rock they were traversing; in fern, horsetail, and sawgrass she might disappear from a predator's eye. At the margin of their range, the two were trying to establish a nesting territory. They needed access to water. Following the mossy scent of a nearby pool, they both broke into a kind of gallop at the splashing sound. They plunged muzzles into the pool, sucked mouthfuls, raised their heads to sluice the water down. The contents of the pool overflowed on down the rocky ledge as they wallowed in to clean their hides and to soak.

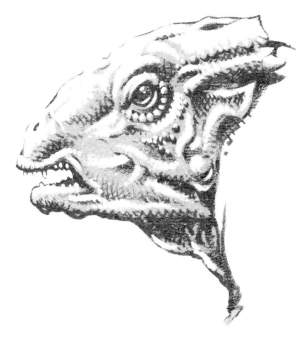

Homolocephale
pachycephalosaur
ornithischian
herbivore
5 ft.
40 lbs.
Upper Cretaceous
Mongolia:
floodplains with
seasonal wet-dry
alternation

The female walked on but then stopped, too bloated to browse the fine greenery sprouting from crannies and clinging to cracks in the stone. She paused until the gutful of water should begin to percolate through her body. She curved her neck to look back along the ledge. The male was paring moss and algae from the wet stones, working his way along until he came to a deep catch basin. In his few seasons, the young male had drunk brackish water from marshes, had drained rain puddles, had drunk from clear creeks and had swallowed mud for whatever water was in it. But he had never seen a pool of quiet water. Slowly raising his head for a moment, he caught the sunset light. The vermilion daubs along his neck glowed. Splashes of light bounced from water and wet rock to play along his skin and heighten the pink swatch on his throat. He bobbed his head to greet or challenge the one just like him in the pool, who did likewise. He cocked his head to fix the rival image with one eye and then the other, and dropped his muzzle to touch noses or to offer a hard bite. The brilliant opposite scattered. He lifted his head. Streaks of bright yellow pollen on the surface of the water and ochre films of the powder everywhere excited his eyes. He puffed out his throat in another challenge, and was answered. Bewildered by the confusion of signals and the other's stance, he backed off only to reapproach and extend his head and neck farther out over the pool, and farther, intending suddenly to hunch back and buffet the other's throat. Both extended, neither would submit. Suddenly he recoiled and struck down: except for a snoutful of water nothing was there, nothing at all. His mate snorted vehemently. He launched himself straight out through the cool water, floundered, dripping, up the other bank and loped on after her.

THE SHADOW

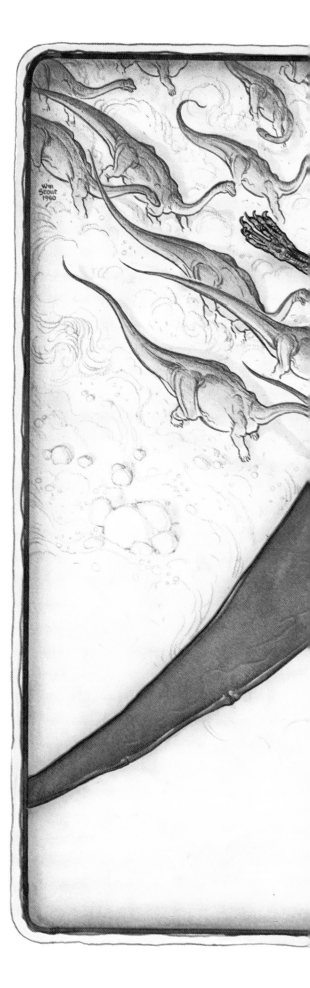

At the top of its flight, each quetzalcoatlus keeps in sight at least one other quetzalcoatlus, at most three or four. Blanked from the sight of others by a cloud, quetzalcoatlus will skim under it, or look for a way around it, or labor to get above it.

The speed and direction of quetzalcoatlus' gliding flight are governed by the interplay of ten or a dozen forces: the wind, updraft or downdraft, big animals on the move, the sight or scent of a ripe carcass, rain columns, fire and smoke, the whereabouts of the mate and the nest, the vector of the sky paths of every other quetzalcoatlus in view, and mood.

For all the glory of its flight, quetzalcoatlus is a scavenger, able to eat carrion too putrid for any other creature with a backbone to eat. This scavenger, alighting on the hill of dead flesh, spreads wings more often than not longer than the head, neck, body and tail of its dead.

Although their bodies suggest mating right at the top of the sky, small hind feet clasping, not belly to belly but joined only where their vents ache and itch, their beaks pointing in opposite directions, wings cocked so that they spin like conjoined samaras down the sky into white bolls of cloud, quetzalcoatlus never developed such practice, and mate on the ground like any great flightless bird.

Although quetzalcoatlus flesh is not eaten, their eggs are, when they can be had. Quetzalcoatlus, therefore, soar great distances to find craggy ledges where they can brood in safety. From such vantage points, a brooding quetzalcoatlus has the climbing egg-thief at a disadvantage, and spears out one eye, or two. Both parents regurgitate for the young.

When quetzalcoatlus is anywhere near the summit of its flight, the bottoms of its up-turned trailing feet, and its back, and the top surfaces of its wings, and the nape of its long, long neck, and the top of its head, and the nasal ridge along its beak—except by another quetzalcoatlus—can never be seen.

Quetzalcoatlus
pterosaur
archosaur
carnivore, scavenger
40 ft.
150 lbs.
Upper Cretaceous
Texas:
floodplain

Alamosaurus
sauropod
saurischian
herbivore
60 ft.
10 tons
Upper Cretaceous
New Mexico, Utah:
floodplain

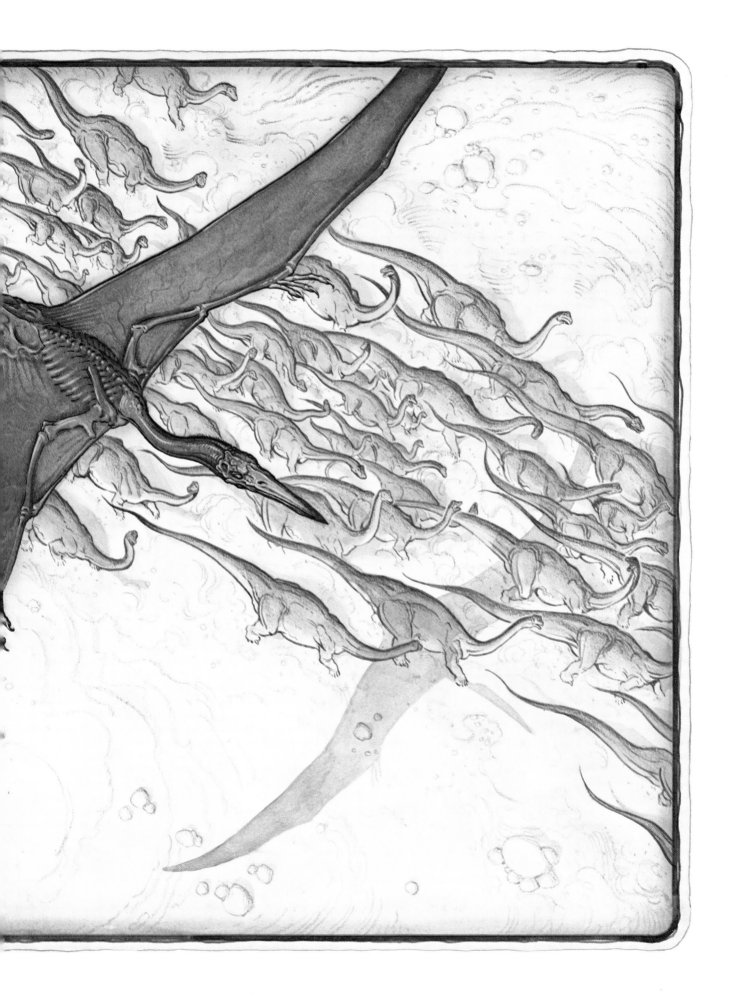

PESTS AND PARASITES

Opposite:

Monoclonius
ceratopsian
ornithischian
herbivore
15-20 feet long
2-3 tons
Upper Cretaceous
Alberta, Montana:
lowland swamp,
forest, floodplain

Below:

Kentrosaurus
stegosaur
ornithischian
herbivore
9 - 15 ft.
500 - 3000 lbs.
Upper Jurassic
Tanzania:
seasonally wet
delta near sea

P lant, herbivore, carnivore— although they may consume one another or be locked in the bitterest competition, the mutual regard they hold for one another is high and intimate. They nourish each other, regulate each others' numbers. In a very real sense, they are blood relatives, including even those in whose vessels what flows is sap. But another set of relationships, equally intimate and of the blood, evokes no such high regard: that between host and parasite, victim and pest. The eye of the warble fly as it hones in on the ceratopsians does not gleam the way the carnosaur's eye does for the same prey. The diplodocus holds worse feelings for leeches than it holds for the crocodilian in the same waters. The cycad palm, cropped and pruned by the kentrosaur, stands healthier than one riddled by beetles. Although the individual dinosaur may have to endure the stings and burns and itches, his tribe as a whole cannot afford the toll of weakness,

disease, and infection which the pests and parasites exact.

Grinding their hides hard against rocks, stumps or each other, the ceratopsians try to ease the maddening itch of fly larvae as they tunnel under the outer skin. Before the maggots can dig too deep, the victims try to abrade the infected areas raw, then scab them over with a coating of dust. Kentro-saurs—one of them having found a deposit of dust of the proper fineness—travel together, a walking thicket of plates and spikes, to ease their misery by rolling in the fine grit which for a while will turn their hides to parched deserts against the small invaders. The treatment is important to them: clumsy as they are, they are willing to roll and wallow, even though this places them at a disadvantage against a passing carnosaur, who understands how long it takes for a kentrosaur to get back on his feet, as does kentrosaur, who does not know for certain how much protection he and his cohort can offer each other in case of attack.

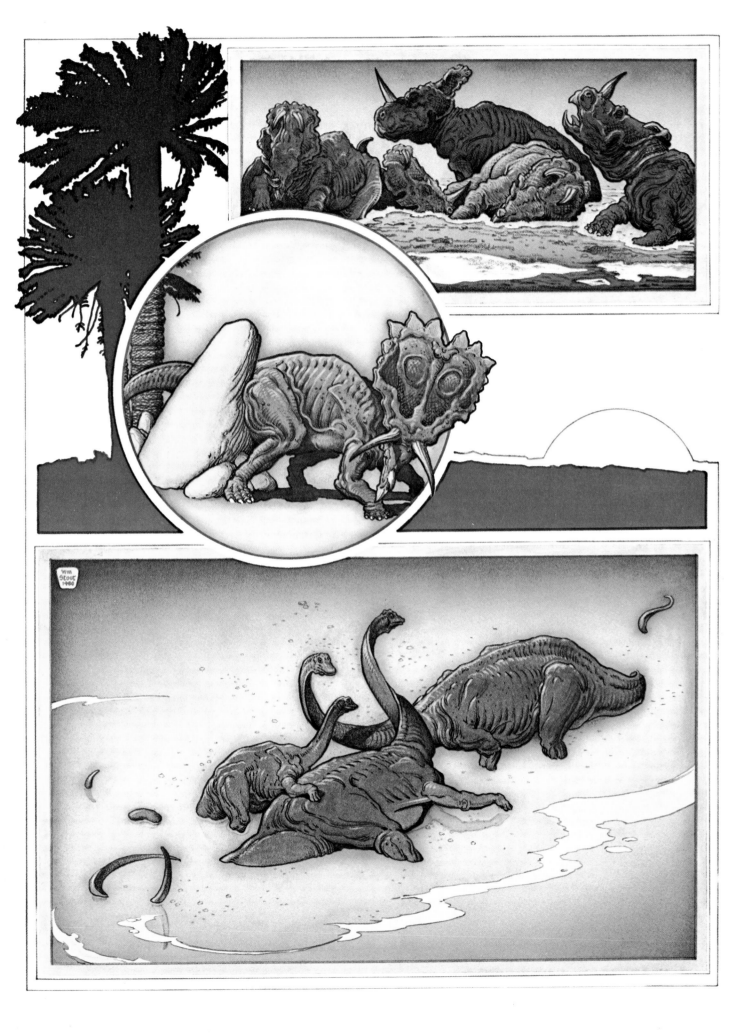

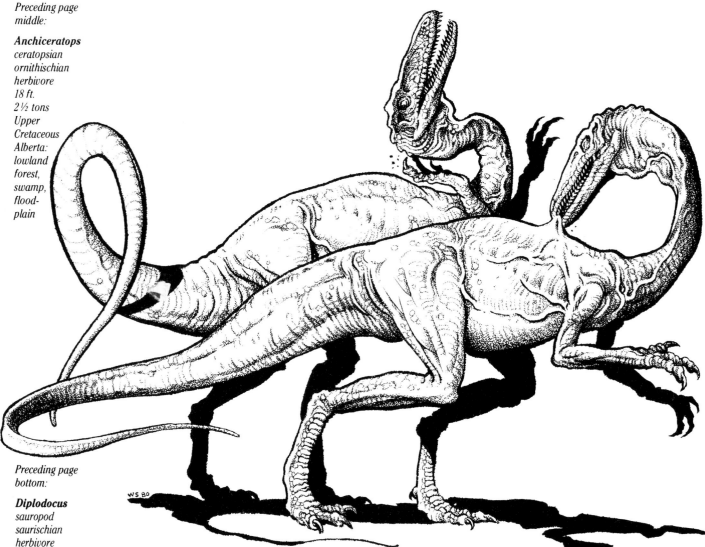

Others resort to mud bogs for relief. The best bogs do more than draw the sting and cool inflammation. The great dinosaurs seek them out, test the shores for firm footing, practice retreats in case of attack, finally back carefully in. Lowing and hissing as the fine abrasive mud balms the lesions, they flounder and roll and submerge. They will risk drawing the easy sinuous approach of crocodilians, not for this immediate relief but for what comes after when, like islands in upheaval, they emerge plodding out from under their own mudslides: the sun bakes the thin coat of mud remaining on their hides to brittle clay which entombs a host of mites, ticks, leeches. The styptic scouring of the clay, as it contracts into shards and falls off, is what the dinosaurs crave, whether or not they know what it does to their parasites.

In bad seasons, the coelurosaurs incessantly pick and snap at their tick-ridden bodies. They run to the water, but the ticks no longer drown, and many of the leeches they attract no longer dry out in the air. The coelurosaurs writhe in sand to scratch places they cannot reach with teeth or claws. One of them spies a fat tick on the ribs of another and impulsively nips it away, pops it bloodily and swallows. A fight almost starts but the other feels the relief . . . . Gradually, throughout the hunting packs and on down the generations, they acquire the humble benevolence of mutual grooming.

BATHROOM HABITS

Coprolites fell, with varying frequency, into two categories: carnivore and herbivore. The former were malodorous, possibly sausage-shaped and, like that of their crocodilian relatives', probably devoid of bone fragments of digested prey. For the carnivore, excretion was an infrequent act, increased only by an unusually large intake of food. Herbivores were generous by comparison. The urge arose frequently, as befitted their enormous consumption. The results were more inflated than the carnivore's, balloon- and pie-shaped, and relatively inoffensive.

A successful, browsing sauropod may have deposited a granular load (filled with tough, undigested seeds) four times a day or more. The undigested seeds buried therein were consequently well-posited for further development: feces were excellent habitat for germination.

Elimination had a beneficial effect on the environment. In defecating, the dinosaurs fertilized the soil, encouraging new growth for later generations of browsers. The banks of lakes, streams, and marshes where hadrosaurs fed may have been lined with abundant, and finely divided plant material expelled by their systems. To the dinosaur senses, there also may have been the faint but acrid smell of ammonia: hadrosaur urine. Dinosaurs in more arid regions, like protoceratops, ejected a dry, pasty white uric acid. Those who favored dry land in humid climates, in fact the great majority of dinosaurs, released a solution of urea. Urine, feces, eggs, and sperm all were released into a common chamber, the birdlike cloaca or sewer.

It is a truism in intuitive physics that what goes up must come down. The biographical counterpart of this dictum is that what goes in must come out. And so it did, eventually; but dinosaurs were no different from all mortal creatures that inhabit the earth. At times peristaltic waves of contraction passed down the colon; cloacas trembled and everted in vain. Constipation struck in the Mesozoic. A hadrosaur was tempted by too much of a good thing: too many oily nuts, too little fiber; a ceratopsian found water less available and its accustomed fodder a little drier; and albertosaur was slowed by cool weather and a painful wound, and so was forced to gnaw dried meat off old bones.

Sometimes what went in was a little surprising: pebbles and stones. Barnyard chickens swallow gravel to help them digest; the gravel in the stomach performs the function of teeth to make up for the lack of them in the usual place. Crocodilians, not being big on chewing, swallow stones, possibly to help mash up prey in their stomachs, but more importantly, to serve as ballast. Dinosaurs had stones in their stomachs, quite possibly to aid in the grinding up of food. Popular theory however, oversteps the known facts in this matter.

Riojasaurus
prosauropod
saurischian
herbivore
7-25 ft.
50 lbs.-2½ tons
Upper Triassic
Argentina:
warm, wet
floodplains
and forests

FRIENDS

In carcasses left behind by packs of hunting carnosaurs, the sharp-jawed larvae of a certain carrion beetle killed the maggots of a certain fly. Some adults of this fly occasionally drilled their eggs into the hides of tyrannosaurs, others were strictly carrion breeders, the rest were indiscriminate. In the intricacies of their adult lives, these flies were their own worst competition: the fading of the carrion flies made room for a plague of tormentors of the tyrannosaur.

Meanwhile, in the lakes and marshes some varieties of the leech which had been prospering on swamp-dwellers had run into trouble as their hosts became predominantly land-dwellers. They subsisted in small numbers, then after some eons found a new world in the very jaws of the tyrannosaurus: They took blood from the gums, settled into the basins under the tongues, cruised the channels between gums and cheeks.

In the most fertile zones, the hunting packs dwindled. Some of their parasites brought disease; infections spread in the wounds caused by others. Maddened, their hunting and mating patterns disrupted, the tyrannosaur packs sought the one relief they knew: the dust baths of drier regions. The fine grit was not a perfect defense against the fly and did nothing against the leeches, but it eased the torture.

Back in the fertile areas, herbivore populations soared. Safe from the teeth of the great predator, all shapes and sizes prospered—prospered too much: woods and swards were shaved down to moss and stubbly fern. The larger browsers starved, their carcasses dotting the terrain from horizon to horizon. Prodigious swarms of insects issued forth from them, fostering multitudes of lizards and birds and pterosaurs. Although some few giant herbivores and predators still roamed the landscape, predominance was taken by thriftier types. The massive carcasses became scarce, the scavenger numbers dropped sharply, and the inflated pterosaur population—all of them slow and ungainly on the ground—found themselves in losing competition with the birds, who were nimble, quick, and precise on the ground. The pterosaurs leaned into the wind, climbed, soared, and, famine on the wing, circled in ever wider circles.

Some of them drifted into the regions where the tyrannosaurs still held out. Some floated down to cling to their rough backs. They were able to pick off only a very few of the huge flies landing to drill their eggs, but whenever the monstrous larvae worked their way toward the ulcered surface to pupate, the pterosaurs plucked them out. Soon they learned to locate their lairs under the raddled skin, which they lanced. The tyrannosaurs bolted at first, but the relief from the deep crawly itch and sting soon induced them to stand still, and to lie and roll from side to side to expose more infestations to the healing stabs.

And then one tyrannosaur, his hide scoured clean, lowered his head toward the ground and swung his jaws slowly open. The single ministering pterosaur kited up, then came back down when he saw the carnosaur not move. He watched the leeches which were dining from the tyrannosaur's gums or plying their ways among the teeth for new sites. Wings half-folded, he hunched

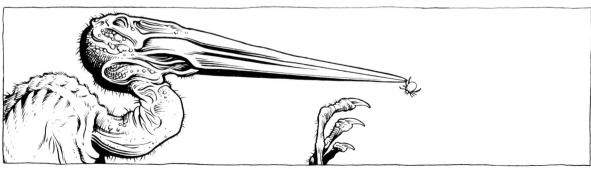

and flopped closer, waited, then proceeded to the brink of the mouth. Bracing on feet and wing-knuckles, the pterosaur shot his head into the maw and out again, rocking back to look at the other's eye. There was no aggression. The pterosaur got into position again and struck: the beak in recoil held one wriggling leech precisely in the point. Ptero-saur took another, and another. A famished flock-mate floated down, dropped flapping for balance next to him and took one leech. Hissing, spreading wings, pecking at his competitor's beak, pterosaur drove the other

away. She ascended to seek out another tyrannosaur....

Purged and healthy, the loose packs began to cohere. The young again tumbled and grappled, set mock bites on each other, and grew fit. Gradually the packs returned to the good lands which were now much changed, and would change again as the overcrowded grazers and browsers found their numbers exposed to the teeth of the great predator. Pterosaur, often clinging to the back of his mount, began to sharpen his appetite for fresh-killed meat and carrion beetles.

Tyrannosaurus
carnosaur
saurischian
carnivore,
scavenger
40 ft.
8 tons
Upper Cretaceous
Montana, Alberta:
floodplains,
swamp forest

A DIFFICULT DINNER

Othnielia slowed down when he came to the bank of a wide creek. Near it, a neuropteron was perching in mid-air. The span of its wings was close to that of othnielia's fingered feet, which spread as he crept up on the dragonfly.

Othnielia flinched just slightly as the snarling buzz of another neuropteron shot past his ear. The two insects then began jittering noisily alongside each other. Othnielia readied himself to snatch both from the air and opened his mouth as they flew toward him. Criss-crossing, they skipped up into higher air to avoid his grasp and resumed their sparring. Othnielia spun and watched narrowly as they zig-zagged furiously around each other. Stalking them, he began to make tiny feints and bobs in time with their maneuvers. One neuropteron broke off and flew right at his eyes. Snatching at it, othnielia nearly caught the other, which had followed. But this was as close as othnielia was to get to them. The two dragonflies resumed their duel, flying out of reach. . . .

In the moonlight, othnielia scouted the border between high marsh and trampled forest. Under an uprooted tree he saw the remains of a really old log; the golden and tan fungi growing out of it showed the neat bites of turtles. Othnielia quietly circled the log: it was too big to be rolled over and still too firm to be torn open all at once. He

sniffed the length of it, listening for the tread of an ant. With a sudden fury of activity, he dug a furrow in close beside it and whirled to strike the scurrying slithering creatures as they fled. He ate the speediest first, the tiny furry ones and the lizards, then a small salamander and a worm larger than the salamander, then white, fat, meaty grubs whose brown heads crunched as he chewed them. He scrabbled around until he found a misplaced edible, a bulky many-colored amphibian with pink gill-feathers and black feet. Few saurians could eat one and survive. Othnielia chomped it twice and got it down. He dug some more, and then began to pick apart as much of the log as he could. He glanced quickly to one side to track the oblivious approach of a single beetle . . . an entire mouthful in one single beetle. Its black body was boldly outlined in white; a bright yellow figure ornamented the juncture where the wing covers met the line of the carapace. The beetle came toward him, its big front legs prancing slowly in the air ahead of it. Othnielia waited, then lipped the beetle up. But before he could bring teeth together, he heard the thing hiss in his mouth. Prudently, othnielia coughed it out . . . entirely too late. He fell to all fours. A putrid fire raced from his tongue to his throat, up the caverns of his head, out his nose. The tubes to his ears burned. The protective membranes of his eyes swept shut as if against a dust storm or the smoke of a forest fire. He

Othnielia
(Laosaurus)
ornithopod
ornithischian
herbivore
3-5 ft.
10-25 lbs.
Upper Jurassic
Utah, Wyoming,
Colorado:
floodplains,
riverbanks

wiped his mouth on the ground: with a swimming motion of his fingered feet he stripped the run of mucus from nose and mouth. He put out his tongue, licked up cool crumbled wood. And then, except for a lingering soreness, the assault on his senses was over. Othnielia did not go back to kill the beetle.

It was a full-moon night, a predator's night. It was time to find cover. First he found a pool. He filled his mouth with water and let it spill out. In the moonlight he pulled the shoots and sprouts which would have to suffice as dinner. Gnawing them, he made for the brake of fallen trees where he would dig in before dawn.

Othnielia slept without recollection of the past day or heed for the next. Somewhere, food would be waiting.

UNDER THE STARS

The crash of trees, the din of cutting, shredding, pulping abates. The herd, skins just touched by shadows and cooler wind, begins to throng: small dense stumpy bodies in the middle, large dense stumpy bodies loosely around the perimeter. The night before, or eons, a carnosaur strode through the formation, seized up the smallest and walked out unscathed. Another night, a similar predator will suffer crippling bites in thigh and shank from jaws which could cut and wrench down a cycad tree. Tonight, however, nothing of the sort will happen.

The young mill in rough, slow circles and for a moment recapitulate—by coincidence or by design—the concentric patterns of their natal clutches. They drift into a copse of palms, press closer, their nubby hides grinding noisily against tree trunks and against each other. Darkness thickens early in the copse. Unable to see clearly, they stop. At first they are so tightly packed that those near the center cannot lie down. After some butting and shoving, all settle down for the sleep.

The rising wind which hisses and clatters through fronds is too cold for the very young to bear alone. While the adults merely shrug their bulks down into the underbrush, five or six small ones, facing windward, stumble around to the lee side of the herd or climb up on top of their slumbering elders to bask in their faint rising warmth. The process goes on all night, the conglomeration mounding up and subsiding but always flowing away from the wind.

Near dawn, with the moon still bright above the horizon, a young male wakes to find his breathing crushed under the heap of bodies, his head clamped, limbs oppressed. His furious hisses are louder than the wind, and the kicking and pummeling of his struggle to escape upward are heard by several night predators, none of whom are drawn to the spot. A few adults wake to the clacking

Protoceratops
ceratopsian
ornithischian
herbivore
18 in.-6 ft.
20-150 lbs.
Upper Cretaceous
Mongolia:
dry semi-desert

of his beak. His dread bites make little or no impression on the thick hides of the victims. Some snap back half-heartedly; others do

not even rouse. Finally the suffocating weight on top of the young male has been dispersed. Front feet on the ribs of a sleeping kin, he stretches a neck too short to stretch, aims a moon-sized yawn skyward, holds it, holds it, slumps back to sleep.

FIRE

T he cycad, grown beyond the reach of the longest neck, is now dying: a smallish bolt of lightning flicks through its dry rosette and down the trunk, which in the bright day glows dull brown orange. After a few moments the tree crumples. The burning crown, flaring as it falls, hits next to the stump. Fitful wind tosses small fireballs at anything which will burn, and two columns of crackling yellow race apart as if the wind were blowing in two directions at once. In the ash-colored sky, bright grey lightning shoots between hanging purple clouds, but it does not rain. Great heavings of wind blow dust, ash, more fire, but no rain.

Some of the animals flee. Reacting to the brightness of the flames, the breaths of heat, and the sight and smell of smoke, many zig-zag crazily, unable to sort out the fires' conflicting messages. Others are able to interpret signals of danger and opportunity. Long-toothed giants keep a safe distance, and wait: in all likelihood, at least one, slower to respond than the rest of its kind, will be trapped and disabled or killed. Nimble coelurosaurs, skirting the fires at high speed, catch small prey as they try to escape.

Stretches of compact thicket spill out swarms of animals usually too furtive and elusive for capture. The coelurosaurs pick up the night wanderers they rarely see otherwise. They swat down the gliders . . . lizards, bend low to scour the ground for whatever crawls or scurries. This happens again and again: a furred animal runs ahead of the flames, sees the coelurosaur coming down on it, darts back until turned by the wall of heat and smoke, whereupon it races into the adroit grasp of the predator. Unless very hungry, a coelurosaur will let drop a caught lizard in order to chase down a prey of redder flesh and richer, warmer blood, and it will scramble, head lowered under the layer of smoke and heat, closer to the fire for such a prey than for any other kind.

One coelurosaur now hobbles like a cripple away from the approaching patches of flame: a broken furred animal hangs from his mouth; in the interlocked talons of his hands another writhes, its jaws snapping; one foot is balled around the body of a third. Slinging his lean frame along, the coelurosaur senses every aspect of the burn he is able to; since he cannot simply outrun the fire with the prey, he lugs along. Unseen behind the smoke, in an intense gathering of fire, a thick fibrous tree trunk hisses out steam and then gas which ignites with a roar some distance from the wood. The startled coelurosaur springs ahead, stops, identifies the sound, goes back for the carcass it dropped.

Coelophysis
(Podekosaurus)
coelurosaur
saurischian
carnivore
3 ft. - 9 ft.
10 lbs. - 60 lbs.
Upper Triassic
New Mexico,
Connecticut:
hot, seasonally
wet floodplain

Icarosaurus
squamatan
lepidosaur
insectivore
12 inches
4 ounces
Upper Triassic
New Jersey
lake-edge swamps

THE NEST

She moved up from the lake where she spent her time simply waiting for something, anything to pass within the arc of the two lightning leaps her stumpy legs could deliver. She bore armor so heavy that a few such charges would exhaust her, and she offered a bite so sharp that a large and lucky victim might escape with a wound almost exactly in the shape of her terrible snout.

She moved from water through ooze, through muck to an area of peaty ground where, bracing with forelegs, she worked her hind pair furiously until a shallow pit had been dug. With mechanical repetition, her body swung left and right to widen it. Sometimes one leg would scoop back in what the other had just scooped out. At last she turned to inspect the dig. She aligned one eye with the moon just clearing the motionless fronds. The light of it pinned her there. Moon,

hole, eye . . . she would wait until the light fell on the bottom of the pit. Should the moon's reflection strike her eye from black water in the bottom, she would quit the site and move to higher ground to dig again, yet she was ignorant that the stagnant water would have putrefied the nest.

This one stayed dry. She waddled heavily off. With all four webbed, taloned feet scratching, raking, kicking, she gathered greenstuff and lined the nest with it. Then she kicked dirt in.

After she had spread one more layer of vegetation in the nest, her body began to convulse, her hind legs to march rigidly in place while she held fast with her front claws. She voided a steaming spew of urine and feces exactly into the nest. In the temporary ease which followed, she gathered more vegetation, spread it, then, raising and dropping her body, punched down a depression under her swollen belly. Another convulsion, an arching of the body, and one by one by one she extruded into the nest gleaming minor moons which seemed to return more moonlight than fell upon them. White mists rose from black water

and swirled, but did not concern her, nor did the soft patter of furtiveness itself drifting through, and returning, and concentrating about her. She spread one last layer of greenery over the eggs, then straddled the nest. Slowly, with snuggling movements, she gently lowered her body onto her own shadow; only her small bright blank eyes, a dome of armor and the jagged serrations along the tail were now visible. Small noises came and went, footfalls and vocalizations.

Before dawn, the nest was steaming faintly around her. A few tendrils of vapor moved in the wind, spread out, a mix of ammonia and shredded fern and a marsh meatiness. Keen noses had long since picked it up.

In the light of paling moon and unrisen sun, they skulked in ragged file into the wide swath around the nest. The mother stayed put. She had learned the futility of giving chase to these furred beasts, whose stench overpowered the rich aroma of her nest. They slouched around her, passing among themselves, heads swinging, tongues lolling out. The mother roared, trembled, shook on the nest, and stayed put: the maternal tie which held her to the nest in terrible conflict

with the frenzy to lunge at her adversaries. She knew they would never attack her. It was her duty to endure their harrassment for however many days until the hatchlings worked their way up through the nest, some to clamp to the skin creases of her legs and neck, others to cluster precisely into her shadow as she strode mightily back into the water; and still others to wander defectively, blindly, in no direction at all or in endless circles until something seized them up in its jaws.

The furred beasts waited, and prowled, until the sun, hot and hazy, beat down on her. In the heat, she might not be able to restrain herself from attack. And so a lone assailant ran in at a back leg. Adroitly she bridged the nest and with a furious sweep of her tail . . . hit nothing. With a rolling cringe, the animal had dodged, melted off into the bush to rejoin those in front of her. As whim or excitement moved them, singly or in pairs they would run in at her, veer off. She treated every sally and fake as death combat, she chomped air, she flailed air. The sun rose in the sky. In turns they slunk down to the shore to gabble up water. Bubbles floated

away from where their mouths had slopped.

They crowded her head, opened up their din. Each time one let out its noise, its entire body would wrack with the effort. They quit when one of their number turned around and, trailing its hind legs like a broken-backed thing, dragged itself off toward the undergrowth with its head skyward to give out warblings of agony. She went for the beast, which at the last moment sprang up and made off. In those seconds, the others with a great commotion ran in on the nest behind her, then dug down hard with fore-paws and bit down repeatedly into the matted vegetation. The mother spun around and charged, her tail lashing so wildly it threw her from side to side as she plunged into the nest. The animals scattered. She stood immobile, slowly spanned four legs over the nest to raise herself clear, then lowered her body into whatever was left of

her brood. She turned her head toward each beast one by one. The few which had got anything slathered their tongues around their chops and almost up to their crowns.

The sun bled orange over half the sky. . . . The pack noticed the exhalation first, long before she did. Now it was their turn to have difficulty in keeping back. The ruined eggs were rotting. The heavy gas would eventually kill any good ones. The mother writhed uneasily, one last time bridged up over the nest. Then, as if she had forgotten why she had waddled up from the lake, and as if the skirmish had never taken place, she lumbered slowly across the swath and through the pack, which gave way pliantly around her. They attended the noise of her slow progress through the underbrush toward the water. Then, emitting noises which were piercing out of all proportion to their runty size, they fell on the nest.

THE MARSH

nder the tall charred trunks of cypresses, a tangled mat of low shrubs and sedge stretched from the river down to the bay. Small herbivores browsed softly. Young ankylosaurs, not yet fully armored, worked on punk logs for the grubs and termites within them. A single hadrosaur swam the river and eased quietly up the bank. She stood upright a long moment, looking around and listening, her nose searching every wrinkle of air. She dropped down to sample what her eyes had already told her was good, then rose up again to give out a series of mellow honks which radiated to the horizon. The signal immediately brought two more to the river and a number down from hill and forest. She stopped honking. Faint answers came from far away. She honked back . . . . The exchange ended only when the farthest away of the group was sure of her location.

Scrawny from a season of drought in the uplands, the families browsed hard through the marsh. The youngest were undersized, and some of them still had to sniff through the greenery beside or behind their elders, tracking their saliva scent for the best forage. The finicky adults, on the other hand, would not take into their mouths anything another had bitten or even breathed on.

They climbed hillocks for the salt brush and the bushes on top, launched themselves into the teeming shallows for the vegetation in either a freshwater current or salt slough nearby or brackish water in between. Terns and gulls rose in clouds to squall down at the hadrosaurs; herons and egrets closed in around them to feed on the winging locusts and scurrying crustaceans they stirred up.

The female who had brought them to the marsh assumed a degree of leadership,

honking to the rest of the herd to announce a bed of sea-wrack or a deadfall of cypress. The others followed her call, or did not, it made little difference; food was abundant. Floundering and wallowing exuberantly, the great bodies filled up. Although a few strides in any direction would yield enough feed for a day, they roved the marsh for variety—and from some ingrained instruction not to strip any land bare. Their slack, dull hides waxed taught and bright, they plunged and cavorted with new vigor. Heralding the mating season, the males tormented the females in the water, bullied each other on land, and brayed all night long.

Their casual leader was in the shallows at the end of a sand spit scooping up kelp, little air bladders popping in her duck bill. With a sheet of the stuff hanging from her mouth, she stopped eating. There occurred some difference in the air scent, a disturbance in the water movement, a change in the bird and wave sounds. The variations were too subtle to alarm her until it was too late. She trumpeted. Not yet touched, the bones of her head resonating with the sound, she trumpeted again. The herd turned as one and propelled itself through water and up muddy banks. Still untouched, she thrashed in the water, trumpeting. At the point of a wake of frothing water, a phobosuchian lunged to fix its final jaws on her neck.

As powerful and harmless as her adversary was powerful and lethal, the hadrosaur reared and plunged into soft marsh bottom, then surfaced, trumpeting again. While the rest of her kind was splashing through shallows and scrambling over hummocks up to dry land, a dozen wakes converged on her, drawn by the tremendous noise, and by the roil of water, and by the tide of blood.

On the following two pages:

Phobosuchus
crocodilian
archosaur
carnivore
40 ft.
2 tons
Upper Cretaceous
Texas:
seashore, lagoons

Kritosaurus
hadrosaur
ornithischian
herbivore
15-30 ft.
1-4 tons
Upper Cretaceous
Alberta, New Jersey,
New Mexico:
floodplains, lakes,
rivers, swamps (i.e.
in and out of water)

Lambeosaurus
hadrosaur
ornithischian
herbivore
12 - 30 ft.
400 lbs. - 3 tons
Upper Cretaceous
Alberta:
floodplains, lakes,
rivers swamps (in
and out of water)

CAMOUFLAGE

THE SEA AND THE STORM

The hunting pack was broken, its members scattered in flight from each other's jaws. There had occurred bad season after bad season, from which their main prey, the sauropod herd, had recovered in individual strength, but not yet in numbers. The skies of those bad seasons, thick with lava dust, by turns sickly livid or refulgent with golds and purples, had finally washed clean, and now, in clear sun from the damp freshly enriched earth, masses of every texture and hue of green were heaving up. Cruising the new growth, each sauropod had waxed sleek, powerful, ponderous with energy. The hunters had been picking their way along behind them, each starved to a ferocity they were too weak to execute. Ahead, no young ones, no ancients, no diseased or feeble: those easier prey had all been stripped away during the seasons of thick sky and little rain.

Persistently following the herd, one or another from the hunting pack would break away to scavenge or to stalk along the narrow muddy shore of the inland sea. To sustain themselves, they would eat young turtles and horseshoe crabs, even wade out to tear at sea reptiles washed up in the shallows, and then return to resume place in the pack. At last the eight or ten carnosaurs simply charged the hindmost of the herd. One of the largest hunters rolled on the ground to try to plunge talons up into the belly of the sauropod, failed, and was walked over, and walked upon. While he was still alive, his cohort fell upon him and tore the stringy flesh from his bones. The hunters' great inhibition, achieved through millenia, was as much as their lack of prey, broken: that, broke the pack.

Through seasons ensuing, the return of other kinds of sustaining prey to the region was so slow that only two pairs of carnosaurs survived. Not vigorous enough to breed successfully, nevertheless they eventually came together. Lethal, fearful, they postured endlessly, going nose-to-nose, threatening, cowering. In turn, each offered bent neck to another's jaws, spun fearfully away, re-offered the neck. At last, registering that the old inhibition was once again in force, they rejoined to become the hunting pack. They set out together after prey.

The spawn of the great thriving sauropods were everywhere, and nowhere. The big hatchlings crowded under the dense deadfalls left by their elders, and disappeared. They sank into mud, and disappeared. They sank into marsh, and disappeared. They crouched among rocks and became rocks. The few that were taken were not enough for the great appetites: the pack sought the adults. In their search, they took the unalert hadrosaur they chanced on, did not try to take the elusive others. A herd of ceratopsians, circling their young, proposed impalement and carnage. The pack went around them . . .

They found the herd as it grazed salt vegetation along the bank of the inland sea. The huge creatures were moving deliberately, now and then inclining long necks to scoop up bunches of seaweed from the water's edge. Between their teeth, the air bladders of the kelpy masses popped noisily between their teeth. The carnosaurs halted. In part driving, in part merely following, they kept after the herd until in the general agitation they were able to single one member out, where the land sloped long and precipitously to the shore. They boxed off their prey, gnashing their jaws together at shoulders and flanks. When the sauropod moved to get back into the herd, the pack bunched up in front of him. When he backed up, they maneuvered for the rolling strike at the underbelly. Pivoting to cover himself with sweeps of his massive tail, the sauropod retreated to the edge of the high ground; undercut, it gave way.

The sauropod kept four legs under him all the way down the earthslide. He stood amid the debris on the narrow beach. The carnosaurs watched. The setting sun dipped into the slot between swollen pendulous clouds and the water horizon: its rays bloodied the

Above:

Pliosaurus
plesiosaur
euryapsid
fish-eater
12 ft.
300 lbs.
Jurassic
Europe:
shallow seas

Centerspread:

Yangchuanosaurus
carnosaur
saurischian
carnivore
Upper Jurassic
China:
floodplains

dinosaurs and whipped the clouds into heaps of pink froth above the opposite horizon. Accustomed to hunting and stalking and killing by sight, the carnosaurs were impelled to bring the action to a close one way or the other. Two went along the bluff, one went a short distance back the way they had come, the fourth stayed put. Then, hooking talons into the crumbly marl, all began to descend the steep cut to the strand. The sauropod swung his long neck and tiny head in all directions for an avenue of escape. He took the only available one, the slivered red path along the water to the sun. The shallow sea roared around his legs as he surged into the water.

The carnosaurs, the striders of dry land, hesitated, then took after him. At first, cranking long legs up clear of the shallow water, they gained. The land began to shelve off, giving the advantage to the tremendous power of the sauropod. He shoved along,

touching bottom with his front legs. The water deepened. Soon all had to commit their bodies to the choppy sea, and, with sinuous sweeps of their tails, they swam. All were essentially out of their element, but the sauropod fled for life while the four hunters persisted: for life, for strength, for growth, and for progeny. They exhausted each other, and bobbed for a while in the swell of the black ocean. They wheezed for air. The hunters tried to close the gap. The sauropod thrashed sluggishly ahead, leaving for them a boil of water. All floated, sucking air. The prey fought to swim clear of them; the carnosaurs wallowed after him. The nearest of them was almost within reach. The long sauropod neck coiled sideways and pressed the hunter's dire head down underwater. The hunter thrashed convulsively. Lacking the instinct necessary to achieve a drowning, the sauropod let the head surface.

The light was gone. In the sudden night,

all sense of land was lost. From between clouds, lightning links shot down icy light. In these jagged moments of illumination, the hunters and the hunted saw their situation, but before they could proceed, they were again in dark water, and could see only soft phosphorescent foam on the low waves. Two hunters swirled in slow circles, trying to locate the land.

And then, the true denizens of the water began to gather. First the pleisiosaurs, eaters of fish and squid. With their dainty jaws and precise little teeth, they could do little, yet sensing the plight of the interlopers, they lazed about in their own wakes of glowing bubbles and waited for blood. Next the pliosaurs, with their shark jaws, and the cryptocleidus, bearers of the ocean's most terrible bite. Chomping watery warnings at each other, they paddled easily toward the intruders. The carnosaurs bit blindly down, kicked land-worn talons in all directions.

Yielding gracefully, the sea creatures cruised the extent of each body. Blasts of light showing only where each sea creature had been, were followed soon by thunder. The pliosaurs and cryptocleidus swooped slowly under each belly, turned and did so again. Then, finally and fatally decided, they executed the screwing half rolls which brought their jaws against the undersides of sauropod and carnosaur alike. The land animals foundered, and when the air escaped from their torn lungs, they sank. The sea creatures fed, and fed, and surfaced for air, and dived spirally down to feed again. Helmeted fish schooled in to nip up small bits, and the pleisiosaurs plunged long necks down for the shreds they had been waiting for. The lightning now is distant, its thunder soft and late, and its light was as dim as the phosphorescence on the waves. Along the bottom of the shallow sea, files of horseshoe crabs converged to clean the great bones.

Above:

Cryptocleidus
plesiosaur
euryapsid
fish-eater
10 ft.
250 lbs.
Upper Jurassic
Europe:
shallow seas

Centerspread:

Zigongosaurus
brachiosaurid
saurischian
herbivore
15-50 ft.
1-20 tons
Upper Jurassic
China:
lake complex

FLIGHT

**Pteranodon
sternbergi**
*pterosaur
archosaur
carnivore
(fish eater)
scavenger
15-27 ft. wing span
15-30 lbs.
Upper Cretaceous
Kansas:
shallow seas*

Whatever it was the flier struck at, struck back, and he went down. Pulled under, bitten again and again, he was left to tumble slowly in the waves, a wrack of torn skin and crossed bones. Blood from the wounds ran in grey threads through the opal water. He ejected the last few fish he had taken that day, one of them still alive to accept the miracle and swim off through a cloud of silver scales.

The flier rolled once and set himself transverse to the waves. From the top of the next surge, pteranodon poked up his long-crested, long-beaked, foam-light head. He worked his wings partially out to embrace the rush of wind. Down in the next trough, and then up again, the peaks of his half-folded wings found air at the rolling top of the wave, but he foundered in the trough again, down. The tiny feet kicked crazily, to no purpose. Above the froth of the next crest, the wings caught enough air to unfold further . . . to spread . . . the flier offered his body down to the water and his wings up to the strong mercy of a wind in which they bellied and flapped to lift the rest of him almost clear of the water. Still kicking crazily, his tiny feet spattered up the face of the next wave and, as if they were doing the whole job, kicked off at the crest. The flier was up.

He struggled for height. The amnesty from pain was quickly ended. The long carpal of the right wing, although not broken in two, had been cracked. He could glide with the wing but to stroke with it was unbearable. The left wing would work, although air streamed bloodily through the ragged tears. On the furred sheen of the topsides of his endless wings were shifting maps of red, pink, coral.

High overhead, his kindred floated effortlessly. Following the schools, riding the winds of day and night, many would touch the water only to feed from it, touch land only to nest. Each noted the broken flapping just above the water, and saw in it a dying cohort.

Awkward, excruciating, seemingly erratic, pteranodon's flight was in fact finely figured. Reading every intention of the wind, he traded distance for altitude or altitude for distance, and one time turned away from land to sail a miles-long parabola into a more dependable current of air. Nearing the home cliffs, his body ached for the casual overnight roosts where others perched for the night. He dipped up a last store of water, shunned the roosts, found the updraft which let him haul himself wing-over-wing in an ascending spiral to the safety of a high rock-roofed ledge, where he and his mate had nested that season. He folded in, landed badly, but was able to right himself and scrabble around to face out to sea, and wait. The bleeding continued. His neck and head lay out along the rock. The clots formed. He roused.

Some of his flock had acquired the practice of feeding any crippled cohort, just as they would a fledgling, and so he called out as a fledgling would call. There was no response. He licked the wounds clean, flexed against the pain of the injured wound, preened and preened. Starvation and healing: the two raced for his life. He spread some wing to catch the warmth of the sun and shuttered down at night. When it rained, he drank the rivulet from the overhang. Luck: he caught a lizard.

Fish, lizard . . . the body went on to burn its miniscule store of fat, then began consuming its own essential substance: tissue to repair tissue. The flier had by now endured more time on that rock ledge than he had spent on the ground all the rest of his life. Finally one dawn, a feeling rose and intensified in him along with the light of the sun: whether fully healed or not, he had nothing remaining in him with which to mend. He could attempt to fly, or he could wait one more day which would be the first of however many it took for him to starve to death on the ledge. Without hesitation, he hopped twice and spread his entirety in the updraft. Tilting this way and that, on some feverish impulse he tucked and slid down the flank of the hill of air and floated euphorically above the low choppy waves.

It was a long way to the fishing grounds. He tried to climb. The injured bone ached

at every beat, but held. In the other wing, part of a long wound reopened, bled. Around the tear, however, the scar tissue held. Weak, without appetite, he flapped, coasted, climbed until the horizon was all ocean.

Specks . . . a column of dowdy-furred juveniles turned slowly above a school of small fish. Pteranodon steered toward them. A last great dome of air: up and over, he dived down the far curve and shot out straight, his juniors yielding with cries of formal protest. He yawed to allow each wave in turn to pass under him, then glided arcades exactly over crest and trough, and when the wind went right, settled into a valley and planed the length of it, inspecting the contents of the water, pale milk of emerald, banked up to either side of him. Weakening, he had to pass by fine fish that he normally could have snatched right up. Once down, he would not be able to get aloft again. He spotted what the juveniles were feeding on, struck, missed. Weaker. Several more of these sprats slid up in the

wall of water to the other side. He tipped one in, lurched. Wingtips whipped water, he steadied. A second, a third. Swallowed. Enough. Their extra weight was pulling down against every wing beat. Nearly powerless, he probed for any fissure in the air which might let him through, veered away from any crease which he might slip down—trifles to the flier healthy. Then, in a perturbation among the wheeling young, he saw the swirl of wind he wanted. He bartered half the height he had won to glide and

bank into it. The swirl carried him up, and up, to a level where he could rest on high rolling cushions of air. Coasting, he drew strength from his catch, watched the dives and splashes of bumptious juveniles and waited for sundown.

Then, seeking the course of his own flock, he tested the strength of the cold sea winds. Exactly in his element, he skimmed the path the others had taken not long ago and flew off to rejoin his mate under billowing clouds perhaps half an ocean distant.

IN THE JUNGLE

The constrictor could wait no longer. He descended the tree and flowed off in the general direction of the faint disturbance which, after wandering closer to the constrictor, was now moving away . . . or might be. The light was growing and things were beginning to show through the thick shadow of ground mist. Unless driven to it, the big snake did not travel on open ground in clear light. Not far from the bole of the tree was the densest of undergrowth, where he would be as safe as in the tree, or in darkness. His head struck out toward it, racing along through great meanders traced, at great length later, by his tail. Between speeding head and tail, the body of the snake was motionless, except for the body's banded markings, which also sped along . . . .

The young sauropod had moved away from the herd in the open forest. The browsing there was meager, and what fell from their cropping activity in the high trees the adults immediately swooped heads down to snatch up. She pushed deeper into the lush brake. Uneasy in isolation, unused to the tangle and snarl of vines and saplings, she craned her head above the mist to scout for danger. As if ducking it under water, she put her head down into the mist, and snatched an entire fern out of the dirt by the base, and immediately raised her head into clear air. The elaborate green tracery of the fern whisked about, bundled, shortened, was gone.

The constrictor moved toward the vibrations of the act, which were stronger than the movement of his scales against brush. Suddenly close, he saw one of the legs, which he registered only as not a tree trunk.

His head stopped short, his body continuing to arrive and fold slowly in behind it. The tongue flicked in and out, in and out in effort to resolve the confusion. Off to one side, the sauropod's small head and serpentine neck came down for another green. The snake punched his blunt snout hard against the side of her head, reared up and set his jaws into the base of her neck. The blow did not stun the young sauropod; her imbedded teeth broke off, but the constrictor held on, got leverage, slid one coil, another, around her body. The sauropod swung around, bit harmlessly. The snake for a moment went lax under the crush of a front foot, writhed free, achieved another coil. Movement stopped. The sauropod exhaled, the snake wound tighter. As if against the weight of deep water, the sauropod took air. The snake had to give her that, but compressed around the next breath out. The sauropod took air once more. The snake was used to having to yield somewhat to the first frantic struggles for air which his victim, suffocating, would make. He was not used to the calm power of the next inhalation, nor the next. The tidal heavings and air told against his own waning strength; that and the strange disparity between the slimness of the neck between his jaws and the gross bulk of the body in his coils, caused the constrictor to slacken. He let go the bite. Tail, hind legs, body, shoulder, one front leg: he flowed through the outline of his own coils back down and off into the mist and tangled brush.

The sauropod twisted her head around to try to pick at the arc of small broken teeth stuck in the hide of her neck, but could not reach them. She set to browsing again.

Madtsoia
25-30 ft.
Nigeria,
Madagascar,
Argentina

Laplatasaurus
sauropod
saurischian
herbivore
70 ft.
20 tons
Upper Cretaceous
South America,
Madagascar, India:
floodplains

UPLANDS

riven by the increase in their own numbers, by famine and by chance, waves of herbivore herds climbed to higher, drier, cooler land, and were followed by their customary predators. Dying out in the harsher climate, sometimes driven out or killed by upland animals more suited to that life, the waves receded . . . and came back again. In receding, eventually, pools of hardier, leaner, more agile, less voracious individuals were left behind, and survived.

Meanwhile, in a single day, in less time than it takes for a carnosaur to crack its way out of its shell, a continent, having strained for eons, cracked the bond and began its journey across half the globe. In some regions, all that showed was a crumbly settling of gravel from which the animals fled. In this upland, however, the split was fatally deep from the moment it opened, was far deeper than that by sundown, and extended from horizon to horizon. And yet a sauropod only several seasons from the egg could step across it that first day, and in so doing cross from one continent to another. Slowly or quickly, however, the gap was widening. . . .

In an upland bend of the fissure, a herd of sauropods milled in agitation, snatching nervously at the high brush as they circled.

Those on the outside craned their heads high, from time to time reared on hind legs as if to feed from high air, then smote earth with great front feet. Wary of those feet, and of the sweeping tails, and above all of the sheer overwhelming mass, a pack of megalosaurs spread out around the herd. Lacking a tactic for singling out one victim, they simply followed the herd, tried false sallies, and waited. The megalosaurs did pick up other animals fleeing out from under the great footfalls. Having chased one such to the ground, torn it apart and eaten it, the largest megalosaur of the pack found himself alone and maneuvering in a continuously shrinking area. Finally, crowded to the very brink of the fissure, he tried to dash through the herd. One sauropod shied massively, collided with another. From the crush, a tail swept, and the megalosaur, battering rock walls, fell.

A rift so sheer, so precise and so deadly steep was entirely new to the sauropod herd. One of them stepped to the opposite wall, missed, plunged and was wedged not far below. Its dying noise panicked another, who also plunged. The rest of the herd, unable to interpret the novel phenomenon of cries from below the earth, skittishly approached the abyss. Lining up there, long necks reach-

ing and bowing as if in a high wind, they attended the noises, located the mangled bodies, scanned the pattern of depth and width. A young one failed to register the signals correctly and joined the two wedged below. The others stayed on, sighting, listening, timidly testing the edge with great broad feet.

In the time that followed, the herd devoured the range down to scrub. The ravenous predators pressed in on the weakened herd and gutted several. One of the lesser members of the herd was the first to try to escape across the crevice. She took the last few steps to it, shuffling on hind legs. She teetered a moment at the edge then dropped to span empty air. Shifting her weight, she stretched one hind leg to meet the front ones on the rim of the opposite continent. She gave a great long shudder of a breath. Sweeping her tail mightily, she carried the other hind leg across and fell sideways just enough across more than straight down to lie in safety. She twisted, gathered her legs, and rose. The herd leader duplicated her feat. Some followed, some balked. Of those who tried, more succeeded than died. One spanned the crevice only to lock immobile. The megalosaurs crowded in and savaged haunches and tail until the animal lurched forward to fall to the quicker death.

The remnants of the sauropod herd, one by one, were cut down and devoured by the pack. The megalosaurs then were left one small isolated region of the old continent with nothing—save only lean upland animals too nimble to catch on scarp and ledge, too small, too elusive or too adroit in herd defense or too exploitive in egg plunder—with which to share their existence.

With a bone-sharp, skull-ringing crack, the fissure walls budged again. Hills echoed back thunder. An unfelt wind moaned the length of the chasm, sending clouds of dust up into the quiet air and then sucking them down again. Light-bodied coelurosaurs and biped herbivores stitched wild zigzags over the rift to find ground which was not shaking under their feet. Pterosaurs flitted between the walls to snap insects stirred up from dead animals at the bottom.

Although it was not yet breeding season, the entire megalosaur pack, large and small, gathered/loosely along the divide and circulated among themselves like slow water beetles on a pond. Each registered that there would be no breeding season. The small, while still fleet of foot, had been unable to catch enough large prey to afford them growth. Those already of breeding size, living on carrion and trying to chase the more

Megalosaurus
carnosaur
saurischian
carnivore
15 ft.
1500 lbs.
Jurassic
Europe:
floodplain, forest,
lake margin

Callovosaurus
ornithopod
ornithischian
herbivore
9 ft.
125 lbs.
Middle Jurassic
England:
wet floodplain,
lakeshore

agile bipeds, lacked the drive and the energy. Across the rift, the wide spoor of the sauropods extended into the low hills and out of sight, but their whereabouts were marked by filttering dots of pterosaurs above them.

The largest megalosaurs followed the divide in the direction of the lowlands whence, generations upon generations ago, they had migrated. From time to time one would stride up to it and crane erect to look for any kind of crossing place for an animal its size. Such was not to be found.

Still in the uplands, the smaller ones simply dispersed. The departure of the adults would afford more prey, the departure of the sauropods ensuring more forage for that prey.

The rest walked about as if aimlessly until, in concert, or perhaps set off by the movement of one, they wheeled toward the rift. Small creatures in their path fled or flattened between rocks. The body and tail of each megalosaur levered up as it gained speed. At the brink, one animal veered and was hit by another behind it. Both tumbled and disappeared. Some at that point drew themselves upright in mid-air to reach hooked talons for rock lip and for life. Some simply lengthened the crucial stride. Some at the zenith of the jump stretched straight out to hurtle their bodies hard onto the ground of the opposite wall. More survived than fell. The largest of them clung to the edge, the talons of his right foreleg clutching a rock on level ground. The hugely powerful hind leg was angled up with the point of one of its talons set into the crack, the others scratching methodically against clean vertical stone. Broken by the impact, the left foreleg was pinned. The talons of the dangling hind leg dug and slipped, dug and slipped. He twisted his neck about to try to bite rock. That failing, he pressed his chin flat against the level ground to try to pry himself up.

The rest of the pack did not recognize the situation, moreover they lacked any method of helping. Accustomed to some degree of leadership from the large one, they came near; not receiving any, they spread out to follow the easy trail of the sauropod herd.

PURSUIT

Right top:

Hesperosuchus
ornithosuchid
thecodont
carnivore
Upper Triassic
Western U.S.

Right bottom:

Poposaurus
poposaurid
thecodont
carnivore
Upper Triassic
Western U.S.

Far right top:

Syntarsus
podokesaurid
saurischian
carnivore
Upper Triassic
Rhodesia

Far right bottom:

Heterodontosaurus
ornithopod
ornithischian
herbivore, omnivore
Upper Triassic
South Africa

T he sun rising above the marsh was so low that even the squat thecodont, hesperosuchus, cast a long shadow: it lunged and engaged poposaurus'. The bodies were apart. In the chill, both animals were sluggish. Thecodont bit; the young poposaur kicked his haunch free before the jaws could clamp. Scrambling back, poposaurus succeeded in making off at a hobbled gallop, at which point another thecodont would have given up. Instead, this one propelled his body up clear of the ground, gathered speed, lengthened his stride, dug more powerfully with his hind legs until his forefeet merely brushed along the tops of low ferns and horsetail.

The young poposaur, already a survivor of many such attempts on his life, was about to slow down. But first he glanced back left, then right, which was why he was not immediately torn apart. He sprang clear of the thecodont's charge. Fleeing across lowlands millennia upon millennia wide, he abandoned his clumsy gallop to run on two legs, leaving other defenses—armor, spikes, a clubbed tail, prodigious size—to others of his kind. Leaner, longer in shank and in stride . . . so too the pursuer, as the generations spun off behind them.

The prey, heterodontosaurus, fled down more thousands of generations and across a barren strew of rocks which the pursuer, syntarsus crossed with equal speed. Each then slipped and slid over mossy stones, down a creek walled by a ravine. Parched, syntarsus stopped to take water. As thirsty, heterodontosaurus hesitated between gaining ten strides and drinking, chose water, nearly lost everything as syntarsus burst out of a cloud of spray and almost closed the gap. Fleeing down the col longer in time than in distance, heterodontosaurus swerved to bound up a rocky avenue into a strip of forest which was not dense enough for concealment nor to confuse pursuit. Forest thinned. They ran out through a new era of shrub and bracken to speed untouchable through a pack of carnosaurs.

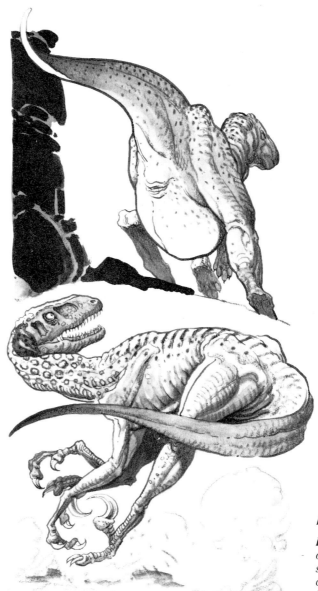

Far left top:

Elaphrosaurus
ornithomimid
saurischian
carnivore
Upper Jurassic
Tanzania

Far left bottom:

Dryosaurus
hypsilophodontid
ornithischian
herbivore
Upper Jurassic
Western U.S.,
and Tanzania

Left top:

Tenontosaurus
ornithopod
ornithischian
herbivore
Lower Cretaceous
Oklahoma,
Wyoming,
Montana

Left bottom:

Deinonychus
coelurosaur
saurischian
carnivore
Lower Cretaceous
Wyoming, Montana

Dryosaurus picked out a hummock in his path, jammed his left foot into it, kicked off exactly to his right. The pursuer, elaphrosaurus, overran the mark, tore up earth to get back in the other's tracks. A spendthrift sprint by elaphrosaurus was matched by dryosaurus, and soon both animals were moving on legs so dead that to force one more stride from them was anguish almost worse than fear or famine. Elaphrosaurus crouched, panting wildly for air. Tracking the other's slow shuffling escape with his eyes, he was driven by an appetite even stronger than his own hunger to rise and pursue. As the chase extended through eon after eon, each began to find reserves never before tapped. The lea flattened and tilted down ahead of them . . .

. . . while behind them, the murky setting sun was still strong enough to throw shadows. They continued, change for change, refinement for refinement, to shape each other. Their shadows stretched many times their own lengths ahead of them. With nowhere to escape to now, no woods or rocks or water, only into ages of flight itself, the prey, tenontosaurus, hurled his entire being into a sweep left and as soon leaned though a sweep right, leaving behind a chute of empty air down which the pursuer, deinonychus, poured himself without losing a stride or gaining. Trying to head off another such swerve, deinonychus gave away his intention: In tenontosaurus's outswelling crystal lenses, in his backward-seeing pupils set in clear amber, deinonychus' tell-tale oblique glance in a certain direction was detected, and tenontosaurus angled lightly off in the opposite direction.

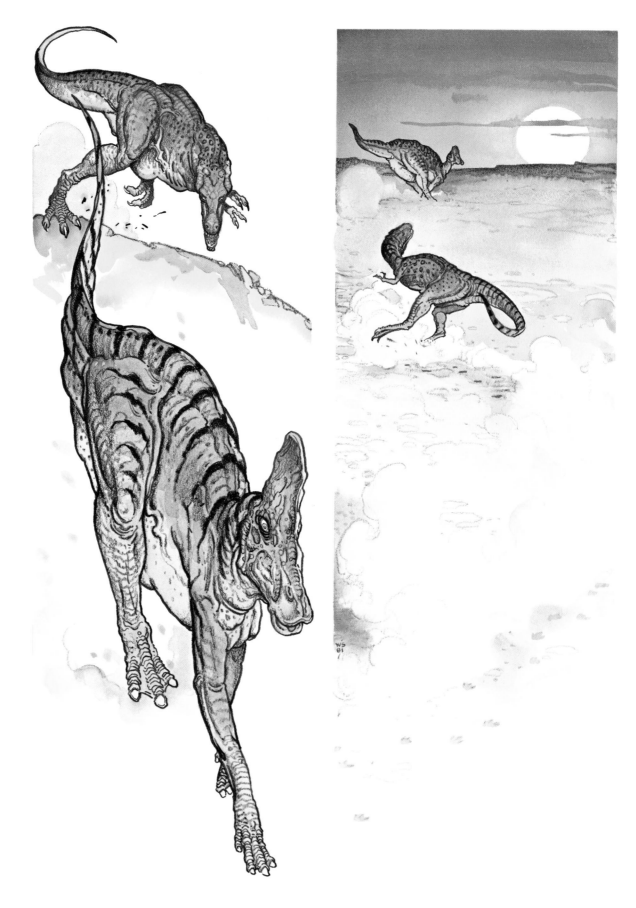

*Right top, and
far right bottom:*

Albertosaurus
*tyrannosaurid
saurischian
carnivore
Upper Cretaceous
Western U.S.*

Right bottom:

Lambeosaurus
*hadrosaur
ornithischian
herbivore
Upper Cretaceous
Alberta*

Far right top:

Hypacrosaurus
*hadrosaur
ornithischian
herbivore
Upper Cretaceous
Alberta*

Albertosaurus fought to recover lost ground. His shadow fell on the back of lambeosaurus, danced forward until it became shadow on shadow, then the shadows whipped apart.

Albertosaurus and hypacrosaurus undulated parallel along the ground, merged, again separated. And so they streamed on and on, ceasing only when the sunlight finally faded.

THE EMBRACE

Smoke hung in the air, and moved. In rock hills, seams blew out: lava flowed briefly, and over it vapor, and gas so heavy in the thick-layered air that it would drift downhill and spread some distance into the lowlands. When the winds came, fires ignited by the lava crossed meadows, sent sparks to forests.

Under the hot haze, a lizard darted from shadow to shadow seeking safety. It was found by velociraptor instead, who chased it down, took it by the neck, and shook it to death. The lizard would be fed to her young, six of them, who would rush at her, pull it from her mouth, and begin to raven it. As the fires had grown worse, food had become a matter of desperation; velociraptor and her brood were starving.

Not too far away protoceratops circled her nest, which she had just uncovered for the day of hatching. Her head swinging, she sampled the air. She could neither identify the peculiar fumes nor determine the direction they were coming from. The only flames visible to her were small, distant, and downwind. Had she been only slightly closer to panicking, she would have trampled every egg and fled. Instead, with the broad side of her beak she began to shove a protective layer of the dry sandy loam back over the eggs. She stopped at the sound of a hit against the inside of shell. And another, and a click and scratch. She raised her head,

stood still. She stood immobilized through a change of wind which brought a wash of fresh air and then an almost unbreathable flow of smoke. Questing the current of good air, she trotted heavily away. Heading toward a wide marsh which had become a stretch of muck among mossy hummocks, she was crossed by an uneasy herd of iguanodons going in uncertain directions. She started to follow them. Not a fire could be seen now, yet the iguanodons had to veer, choking, from a rolling front of fumes. Protoceratops went in the opposite direction, returning to her nest, which the starving velociraptor had already found. With a threatening squeal, protoceratops charged the plunderer, who did not look up. Gobbling newborn and shell together, velociraptor made no attempt to evade the leap at her neck. The mouthful was coughed out. Then velociraptor twisted what she could of her supple neck to savage back at her assailant, and raked sharp talons into her underbelly. The beak was grinding deeper into velociraptor's neck when, like an almost invisible surf rolling in, a wave of gases, just thick enough to cause the horizon to shimmer, covered them. One breath made the adversaries convulsively kick loose from each other, the next two brought them slumping slowly together to fall into the nest. Gradually the wind picked up, and roared, then at sundown ceased. Soft ash began to cover them.

Protoceratops
ceratopsian
ornithischian
herbivore
18 in.-6 ft.
20-150 lbs.
Upper Cretaceous
Mongolia:
dry semi-desert

Velociraptor
coelurosaur
saurischian
carnivore
8 ft.
150 lbs.
Upper Cretaceous
Mongolia:
dry semi-desert

THE NOSE

The loudest sound, the sough of young camarasaur's breathing, is not loud enough to cover the busy suck and slurp of her feeding on the water greens—salvinia blanketing the top, endless streamers of anacharis just below, and rolling clouds of water meal gleaming like sand of emeralds—which muffle any turbulence from her slow way. Even while she ejects a mouthful of water from which the greens have been strained, the breathing continues through the nostrils high on her head. Her body sinks slightly with the exhalation, bobs up as she takes air in. Like a separate creature, her head and neck snake from side to side to gather in just as much as she can possibly process.

Pushing along when she can touch the oozy bottom, oaring with her tail when she cannot, she nears the trunk of a great tree fallen across the water. An eye in that formation opens and the shape of an enormous crocodilian appears around it. Camarasaur drifts to a stop, breaks wind, the bubbles rising to join the wafts of marsh gas over the water's surface. The crocodilian, basking on a gorged stomach, will not go after her; its eyelids close. Camarasaur, with slow sinuous curves of neck and tail, propels herself backward, turns, circumvents the tree, cruises on through the days . . .

If attacked by an aquatic predator, she is without immediate means of defense or escape. Her survival depends on growing large enough to safely travel on land where her great size can join the others of her herd to form a protective whole—sheer immensity in motion. As she wades or swims through the seasons, now and then lumbering up to dry land for extra forage, her neck lengthens in proportion to her growing body. If the aquatic pasture, ravaged by camarasaur and her kind, should give out, she would have to take to dry land prematurely. This time, wetlands vegetation is sustained and so one day camarasaur, festooned with greenery, plods up toward firm ground. Seeking the protection of the fully grown amassed in a herd, she moves unceasingly, like the rest of her generation. She soon registers that she is on the trail of a herd as she comes to trees stripped of their bounty above the reach of her neck, and above what she can reach even when braced on tail and hind legs. Consuming some few leaves remaining on scattered branches, camarasaur continues her quest for the protective numbers of the herd.

Camarasaurus
sauropod
saurischian
herbivore
15-65 ft.
1-25 tons
Upper Jurassic
Western U.S.:
lake complex

EYES

T he eyes of the little fabrosaur are pools of gold surrounding deep black, perfectly round pupils. They gaze out languidly over the dry floodplain. A gust of wind kicks up dust, and a flinty sliver lands in fabrosaur's left eye. He is disadvantaged at being so small: fabrosaur's eyes are so close to the ground that these mishaps happen frequently. Tears well up, and the rusty brown lower lid, stiff and scaley, rises up on its own impulse to close against the upper one. Simultaneously, the thin, almost transparent third eyelid flicks backward from the forward angle of the eye and shepherds the offending object toward the rear angle of the eye. As the lower lid drops and the third eyelid returns to its inconspicuous seat, the sharp stab of pain dulls. The flow of tears continues for a bit, and fabrosaur worries at the corner of his eye for several minutes with clumsy sweeps of his small, clawed hand. Either by the flow of tears or by the action of his paw, the troublesome sliver yields and returns harmlessly to the ground whence it came. Greatly relieved, the fabrosaur resumes his surveillance. To survey the distance ahead of him, he slowly pivots his neck to the left and right . . . Dinosaurs' eyes, mounted on the sides of the head, afford a wide sweep, but are not set for looking straight ahead, hence the existence of various flexibile necks and mobile heads.

Although all seem tranquil in the hot, midday doldrums, fabrosaur catches sight of a sulphur-yellow patch of color in motion along the crest of a distant ridge. The patch, the trace of a fleet-footed predator, disappears. Not waiting to find out if he had been seen in turn, and using his tawny color as camouflage, fabrosaur skitters away down the long gray gully in the opposite direction.

Color vision and night vision are more or less at odds with each other. During the Age of Reptiles, mammals, small creatures that they were, cowered in holes or up in trees by day and ventured abroad only by night. They developed keen night vision, but at the expense of their ability to perceive color. Thus, they are a drab lot of animals even today—dominated by black, gray, white and brown (primates re-invented color vision—but monkeys, apes and man are but a tiny portion of the mammalian assemblage). The vibrant colors of the natural world are meant for eyes that can appreciate them, animals that are abroad by day: insects, birds and reptiles, for instance. Dinosaurs walked abroad by day, they saw color, they used color. They attracted mates with stunning chromatic displays, they warned would-be predators of the unfortunate consequences of foolish attack with harlequin warning patterns. Dinosaurs were eye-dominated creatures. In general, predators had larger, keener eyes than their prey. Ornithomimids were ostrich-sized, toothless eaters of animal protein. Their eyes were a third again as large as those of large-eyed ostriches that grace the African plains today. They, as well as certain other exceptionally large-eyed small predators like *Stenonychosaurus*, may have stalked warm, furry prey in the dim light of dawn or the fading light of dusk. Night eyes of most land animals (owls are an exception) have vertical, slit-like pupils and shiny-reflective layers that coat the retina, gathering whatever dim light is available. Hadrosaurs in many ways form the summit of dinosaur evolution, the product of more than a hundred million years of saurian "better ideas." As befits large, day-living animals who were accustomed to receiving colorful visual signals from each other and to sensing predators from afar, hadrosaurs had large, keen eyes with correspondingly developed visual centers in the brain. Their eyeballs measured up to three inches across—half again the size of a horse's eye; and the horse is said to have the largest eye among mammals.

Big eyes, little eyes; brilliantly hued eyes, cold gray eyes; round-pupiled eyes, slit-like eyes: it was a world of colors—and eyes for seeing them.

Fabrosaurus
ornithopod
ornithischian
herbivore
3 ft.
20 lbs.
Upper Triassic
South Africa
dry floodplains

HIGH FASHION

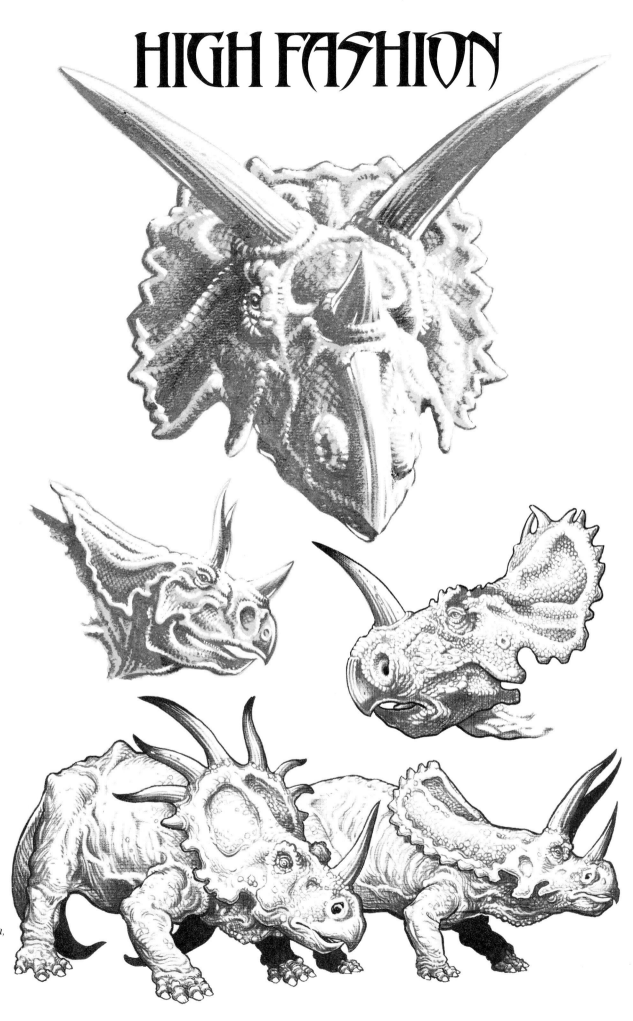

This page
clockwise:

Arrhinoceratops

Monoclonius
ceratopsian
ornithischian
herbivore
15-20 feet long
2-3 tons
Upper Cretaceous
Alberta, Montana:
lowland swamp,
forest, floodplain

Pentaceratops

Styracosaurus
ceratopsian
ornithischian
herbivore
10-20 ft.
1-3 tons
Upper Cretaceous
Alberta:
lowland forest,
swamp, floodplain

Eoceratops

Opposite clockwise:

Chasmosaurus
ceratopsian
ornithischian
herbivore
15-20 ft.
2-3 tons
Upper Cretaceous
Alberta:
lowland swamp
forest, floodplain

Anchiceratops
ceratopsian
ornithischian
herbivore
18 ft.
2½ tons
Upper Cretaceous
Alberta:
lowland forest,
swamp, floodplain

Triceratops
ceratopsian
ornithischian
herbivore
20-30 ft.
4-6 tons
Upper Cretaceous
Wyoming, Montana,
Alberta:
floodplains,
swamp forests

These head-pieces evolved from a simple helmet designed to protect the skull and nape into an almost heraldic device of the era—a device for disembowelling the foe, dazzling and delighting the onlooker, and discouraging the competition.

The angle of an animal's horns tells us something about its tactics against rival or predator. The bull and bison hook, the ram smashes head-on, while the goat and gazelle have two modes: a blunt, often ritualized blow to a rival's casque and a backward stab on the back or flank. The herbivore's defense need not be lethal, nor even successful every time, to register in the course of thousands of generations; a single puncture or gash may suffice. On the other hand, many styles of horns and antlers have flared, curved, spiraled and enlarged with more of an eye for attracting the female than for inflicting great damage. Although the proliferation of ceratopsian styles—the size and shape of the bony frill, the number and length and location of the horns—suggests an almost frivolous indulgence in the possibilities of genetic variation, the function of the apparatus was entirely straightforward. Yet the key to later ceratopsian success probably was protoceratops's simple arc of bone, serving to spread the origin of the masseter (the muscle for chewing), which enabled the creature to exploit the availability of tougher, coarser vegetation with increased leverage.

PLATES

tegosaur is hungry. He sees a clump of green tight-curled leaves. He goes to the clump and tries to eat it. The green is tough, dry, bitter. Stegosaur moves on. He sees the high tree fern he knows is good: he ate from it the day before. He walks his front feet up the trunk but there is little foliage left within his reach. He kicks off, lands heavily on his front feet. Brushing through dry bracken, he sees green growth with small bright fruits in it and eats it to the stump. He sees another clump of green tight-curled leaves. He goes to the clump and tries to eat it . . . stegosaur does not learn quickly.

Stegosaur moves from the heat of a broad glade into the cold marsh to browse the water plants. His body is soon chilled. The plates along his back, which have been extended sideways to shade his flanks from the overhead sun, now go up. In sunshine, the blood supply to the plates is constricted so that the blood flowing through them will not overheat his body. In cooler times, with the plates upright, more blood can flow through them to bring the warmth they have collected into stegosaur's flesh. Mornings, the plates also rise to catch the sun and so stegosaur gets an early start on the day. Afternoons, if overheated, stegosaur can amble into the shade where the plates will radiate some of the excess heat away, all without stegosaur's having to think about it.

Stegosaur's plates are also useful in signalling arousal between male and female. And useful now to ward off even the dread allosaur: the plates spring up and stegosaur flares almost twice as big as before in allosaur's vision.

The plates remind allosaur of a previous encounter with stegosaur's spiked tail and he is dissuaded from attack. He no longer strides, he hobbles. A deep triple puncture in allosaur's thigh from stegosaur's tail had become infected, healed badly. Another time, another strike, stegosaur's barb had ruined one eye and damaged allosaur's hearing. Lesser scars mark allosaur's body.

Allosaur does not learn quickly, but he learns. He moves off to hunt elsewhere, but is unable to find simpler prey and in desperation circles back to find stegosaur. This time when the plates spring up allosaur is not warned off. He is too hungry. This time he is warned to dodge the spiked tail. . . .

Stegosaur will die without issue. Long before the time comes for other dinosaurs, his line will be discontinued. Compared to them, he may be too slow of foot, too slow of wit. His plates may be too cumbersome a device for the milder climates. Or perhaps his disappearance may have nothing to do with these factors.

Allosaurus
carnosaur
saurischian
carnivore,
scavenger
8 ft.-40 ft.
100 lbs.-4 tons
Upper Jurassic
Wyoming, Colorado,
Utah, New Mexico,
Oklahoma:
wet and dry
floodplain, river
and lake shore

Stegosaurus
stegosaur
ornithischian
herbivore
4-20 ft.
40 lbs-3 tons
Upper Jurassic
Wyoming,
Colorado, Utah:
floodplains,
riverbanks,
shorelines of lakes

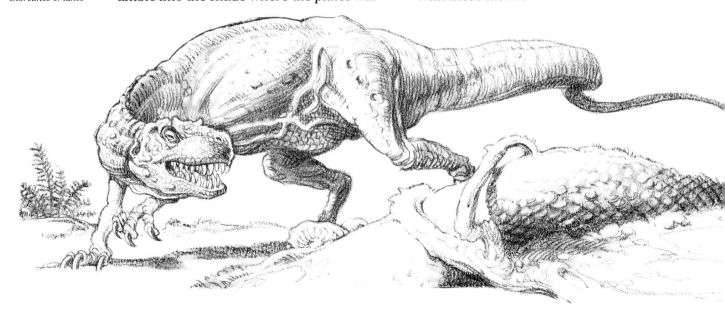

CLAWS

Deinonychus, in a rage of thirst and hunger, was soon to be driven to the kind of minor mistake which could have incurred his death, but which he would survive. Ravenous from many consecutive days of eating lizards too spindly for his great hooked claws, and of eating carrion deteriorated long past the need for any such weapon, he caught sight of a fat amblypod hiding among rocks. A few hurtling leaps took him to it. He plunged one curved hook down, hit rock, then threw himself headlong to seize the scrambling prey with foreclaws. But as he tore the small fat thing apart with his talon, the pain began: deinonychus' claw had been broken. In a good season, the pith would have sealed over quickly and a new point formed. This time, however, the depleted animal's claw became infected. Deinonychus kept it cocked up carefully as he hunted and scavenged. Limping then, but not crippled; hungry, but not starved; hurting, but not debilitated; deinonychus survived day by day, like his kind. Victims of their own success, they had hunted their select prey down to a scattered few. Now they were either seeking out petty game, facing larger animals in aggressive herds or chasing smaller bipeds as fast or faster than themselves. . . .

The thud of foot on ground, the scratch of talon on stone, the hiss and rush of breathing drew him. Seeking a share of a kill, or all of it, he came upon another of his kind, a scrawny concatenation of claws and teeth who was breaking off from charge after charge at an iguanodont, half-grown but formidable, with heavy-clawed feet and spiked hands and a big bite, and as large as the two predators together. Deinonychus watched blankly until his counterpart, an undersized female, began to give up. When she retreated, deinonychus saw the prey turn her vulnerable flanks toward him. Numb to the pain of the infected foot, he rushed in. The female saw the dash as an attempt to snatch quarry from her, rushed in also. The iguanadont wheeled to grapple the first, saw the next, tried to run. . . .

They were at first too ravenous to quarrel over the kill and finally too satiated. In the following days, they made only short forays away from the precious carcass, returning to strip it in the evening, and to ambush scavengers. When the meat gave out, they moved off together into a terrain as unsparing as they themselves were.

Although the sun no longer heralded a breeding season, during which the female had been too meager to form eggs, some residual currents flowed between these ungregarious predators. Hunting prey, in the final dash each saw the other as a competitor trying to run past and bear off the kill, and yet together they brought down animals neither would have attempted alone. Then, while one was gnawing flesh from bone, the other would to some slight extent drive off or spear scavengers who would thieve their store. However slight, that extent gave them a great edge.

When breeding season came again, they mated after an entanglement of hooks and bloodless clash of jaws. The ensuing clutch of eggs they guarded diligently enough to drive off marauders until the eggs hatched, whereupon they left the young to their own devices.

Some seasons later, the female, struggling against the pain of her joints, and the male, with one sound claw and the other healed back to a spiked stump, were working to keep a resourceful and bellicose ornithischian clear of the cover where the rest of its herd waited. The big animal was not trying to drive them off or to flee: it maneuvered so as to let the two deinonychus close in so that it could mangle them with tail, feet, or heavy jaws. The two looped and weaved around each other again and again until the ornithischian, tiring, began to angle toward the thicket.

A noise behind them: springing past, several in a troop, one last one slower, more of them, with high-thrashing legs and footfalls so precise they did not kick up dirt or gravel, all with perfect curved talons and unworn teeth. The two deinonychus did not recognize them as their first brood but only as competitors attempting to snatch a prey from their mouths. The two raced the younger ones in. The ornithischian whirled, slowly, to try to front the claws which leaped up at it. Only those to the rear and at the

Deinonychus
coelurosaur
saurischian
carnivore
8 ft.
150 lbs.
Lower Cretaceous
Wyoming, Montana:
dry floodplain,
riverbank

Tenontosaurus
ornithopod
ornithischian
herbivore
4-20 ft.
40 lbs.-3000 lbs.
Lower Cretaceous
Oklahoma, Wyoming,
Montana:
dry floodplain,
riverbank

flanks climbed, dug in . . . kicked clear when the ornithischian rolled, again climbed on, and sank claws in. The throes grew more violent, less directed. The troop now waited on the ground until merciful lethargy calmed the bleeding animal, and then fell to.

Deinonychus
coelurosaur
saurischian
carnivore
8 ft.
150 lbs.
Lower Cretaceous
Wyoming, Montana:
dry floodplain,
riverbank

T he few predators which in past eons used to try to attack deinonychus have died out or given up, blinded, or with throats torn, or bellies ripped. Against ordinary prey, deinonychus springs high to bring the animal down with kicks of sickle-clawed hind legs. Against herbivores larger than himself deinonychus rolls supine to degut with a flurry of upward kicks.

Although from horizon to horizon and beyond there is not another male of the race, these two stand against each other to duel for it all. They measure each other. Each extends his body just above the ground. A flex of tail levers each deinonychus up. They kick so fast that their sickle talons chirp in the air. They bob heads slowly, almost nose-to-nose. Suddenly, with volcanic hisses, they display teeth and jaws which could tear out each other's throats with a bite. The intensity of saurian fear and fury becomes almost palpable with the realization that each is virtually defenseless against the other: there exists not a knob, spike, bony mass, or plate of armor between them. Neither can turn tail and flee without exposing his body to lethal attack. They seem locked into fatal encounter. They charge, flicking blades at each other's flanks

menacingly in passing. Each does have this one way out: after the charge, he could keep right on going. The option is scorned. They pass each other again and again, the fury mounts, they score double furrows in the earth before charging once more. They come slowly at each other in weaving diagonals, and clearly the final clash in imminent. In this phase, the half-step backwards one takes is as ominous as the other's show of teeth. Close now, they orbit a center point. Knuckles of their murderous front hooks drag almost casually along the ground, then each strightens up somewhat . . . And suddenly it is over. There has occurred a lightning strike, yet there is no blood. One deinonychus has seen in the other's moves something final and fatal and unpreventable, therefore he resigns while his body is still intact. At no point have the adversaries even touched, for to have done so would have triggered an irreversible attack from which neither could have walked away . . . except into days of blood loss, infirmity, gangrene . . . decline, and death. So one deinonychus flares the vulnerable curve of his belly to the victor's forebearance—who crouches, head bobbing, to wait while the loser gets out of his sight while the getting is good.

THE TONGUE

T wo pelorosaurs are feeding, an adult and another, not shoulder-high to the big one. The adult stretches his long sauropod neck up into a tall cycad, nips and pulls. He retracts his neck and head from the crown of the tree: feathery fronds of cycad adorn his face. As he bites, the green that is outside his mouth flutters down to the ground, where the smaller creature stoops for the gleaning. Several nimble ornithischians dart in triumphantly to snatch most of it away—vegetation which otherwise they could not reach.

The pelorosaurs swallow their mouthfuls without chewing and get on with the task of satisfying their huge and growing frames. Lacking cheeks in which to put their harvest, or tongues to move it around in their mouths, and having only simple teeth with which to chew, the pelorosaurs are not effi-cient in their browsing, and sustenance is tough for them.

Nearby, an old iguanodon is phlegmatical-ly chewing his green stuff. Not everyone in his community can go along with his choice of fodder: tough fibrous leaves which other dinosaurs—like the speedy little hypsilopho-don or the low lumbering ankylosaur—are ill-equipped to process. Yet the iguanodon's food serves him well. His chewing now ceases: his cheeks are filled with finely com-minuted plant debris. As his jaws part, his heavy fleshy tongue moves to the left and plunges into the trough between cheek and toothrow which has captured the saliva-soaked plant material and kept it from spill-ing onto the ground. Reflexively the tongue ploughs forward in the furrow, then flicks the gruel back into the mouth. The jaws close, the throat tenses and rises. With a soft, deep-pitched gurgle and gulp, the green bolus tumbles down the esophagus into the iguanodon's bowels. Automatically the tongue proceeds to ream out the cheek trough on the other side. Contentedly arch-ing his neck once more, the iguanodon protrudes his tongue, gathers fresh leaves towards his mouth, retracts his tongue, nips off the leaves between the horny rasps of his toothless beak and starts chewing once again.

Iguanodon
ornithopod
ornithischian
herbivore
15-30 ft.
1-6 tons
Lower Cretaceous
England, Belgium:
swamps beside large
lake complex

TEETH

Top:

Gracilisuchus
thecodont
archosaur
carnivore, insectivore
2 ft.
2 lbs.
Upper Triassic
Argentina:
wet floodplain

Middle:

Dinodontosaurus
dicynodont
therapsid
herbivore
5 ft.
100 lbs.
Middle Triassic
Brazil, Argentina:
wet floodplain

Bottom:

Lagosuchus
thecodont
archosaur
insectivore
18 inches
1 lb.
Upper Triassic
Argentina:
wet floodplain

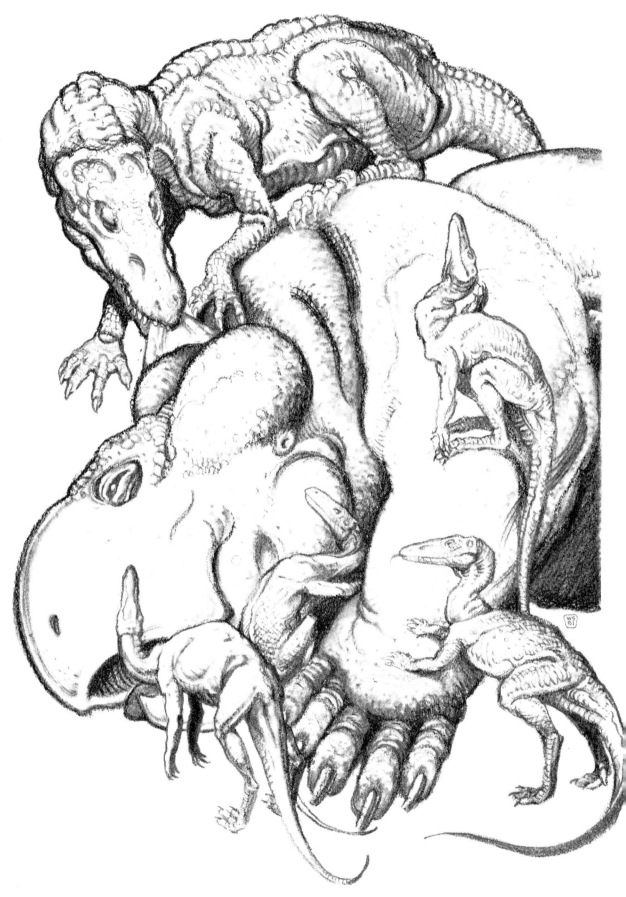

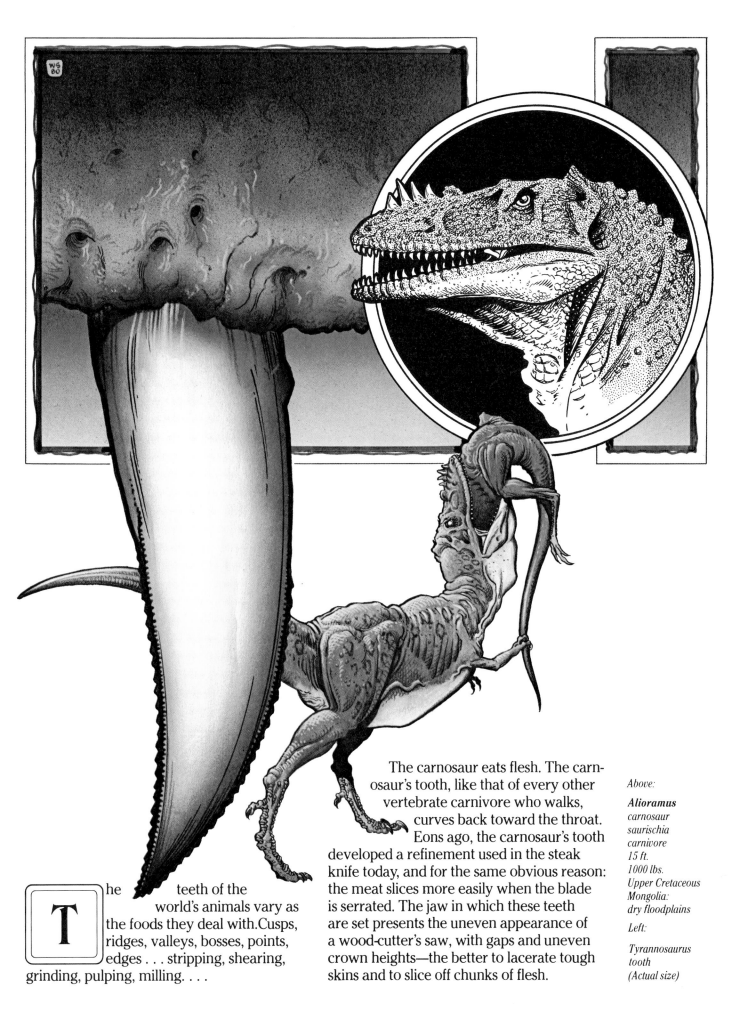

The carnosaur eats flesh. The carnosaur's tooth, like that of every other vertebrate carnivore who walks, curves back toward the throat. Eons ago, the carnosaur's tooth developed a refinement used in the steak knife today, and for the same obvious reason: the meat slices more easily when the blade is serrated. The jaw in which these teeth are set presents the uneven appearance of a wood-cutter's saw, with gaps and uneven crown heights—the better to lacerate tough skins and to slice off chunks of flesh.

The teeth of the world's animals vary as the foods they deal with.Cusps, ridges, valleys, bosses, points, edges . . . stripping, shearing, grinding, pulping, milling. . . .

Above:

Alioramus
*carnosaur
saurischia
carnivore
15 ft.
1000 lbs.
Upper Cretaceous
Mongolia:
dry floodplains*

Left:

*Tyrannosaurus
tooth
(Actual size)*

SPINES

Spinosaurus
carnosaur
saurischian
carnivore,
scavenger
30 ft.
3 tons
Upper cretaceous
Egypt:
wet floodplain

I t was always dead cold at sunrise. At the first flush of orange light, the long folded spines rose to spread the skin between them. Through those membranes the dawn light shed its warmth, glowing in cool streams of green and purple. Spinosaur yawned his jagged mouth, waited for the warmth to flow down into his whole body.

Fleeing the strange, cold, murky skies, following the retreat of good forage, all kinds of herbivores had begun to wander into spinosaur's realm, and with them came the meat-eaters from those disrupted climes.

Inured to only the cool of a night and the heat of the ordinary day, both suffered in the region's daily swing from pitiless sun to lunar cold. By day they lowered themselves into the scant streams and the water holes, straying only to hunt or to forage in the shade. At night they groveled down, shivering, into the pebbly earth, and often could not rouse the next day before too little of it was left for them to make up the energy they had lost. The meat-eaters, of such present size and previous voracity that they could have broken spinosaur's neck with a single bite and

shake, now were too feeble to do more than scavenge. The herbivores were mightier than anything else in spinosaur's experience, he never would have attempted one were it not that they all were weakened: the new region's tough scant forage and bitter climate were inhospitable to their kinds. Spinosaur throve on the abundant prey and fattened from the ease of the predation. He no longer pursued what had been his fit prey, a rangy hadrosaur, who also bore along its back the same kind of fin. Both animals spread it for morning warmth, and later, in shade, for whatever fanning wind there was to flush the paralyzing heat from their bodies. Matching each other in vigor, hadrosaur and spinosaur pack had kept each other perpetually fit until now. As spinosaur abandoned such tough game for the easy pickings moving in, the hadrosaurs began to strip the lean land. . . .

Spinosaur was warily circling a dying carnivore: this prodigious invader was easier meat than a vigorous hadrosaur. Crushed by the sun, it gaped horrific jaws merely for the cooling air over damp tongue, gums, cheeks. When those parched, its jaws slowly shut. Spinosaur was searching out the spot for the safe death bite. He crept past the neck to the closed jaw, the closed eye. The lower lid slid down, the upper rose. Around the full black disk of the pupil, amber filaments of the iris streamed. In that pool, the small bright inverted image of spinosaur shone back. He froze, he neither twitched nor breathed as

slowly the pupil began to contract from
round down to a tight and malign slit of an
ellipse. The lids moved to meet each other,

snapped open before spinosaur could move,
but when they again moved and closed,
spinosaur this time was ready, and fled.

BONES

Although the sun was still high, the bottom of the defile was deeply shadowed. The troop of ankylosaurs moving through it was not strung out single file, but stayed three and four abreast. Crowded close together, they snapped irritably at each other and lashed out with their clubbed tails. In the lead was the oldest female, still vigorous; next, an old male; then some juveniles. The female halted. One member of the group advanced past her, stopped, swung his armored head—nearsighted but keen of ear and nose—and grunted. Another pressed on past him.

In the dry silt they were traversing, there was nothing at all to eat. The upland meadows they had left had become lean of forage and beset with predators and scavengers who in famine were banding together to kill. In those same meadows, however, there were still suckering stumps to browse and rocks and logs to turn. Unaccustomed to, and physically ill-equipped for, migration, the ankylosaurs thus felt the urge to retreat to what they had left only that morning. But they did not.

They came to where the deep fissure had captured a creek. It fell from high overhead, spattering into bright spray against rocks, threading on down into darkness and a pool which overflowed into a rill running on ahead of them. The ankylosaurs clambered over each other to drink. They dug into the low banks for shellfish and larvae, found nothing and turned rocks which yielded only a flow of muddied water.

The oldest female, her consort, then the juveniles, plodded ahead. The rest of the herd blundered about before following. The defile, changing direction, caught full sun down its length. Insects danced in the rays. Ferns in high crannies blazed green. Below was still barren. The lead group kept going, the others dragged on behind them. The defile turned, the ankylosaurs marched again through shade. The rock walls opened out a little, and the old female halted: a massive drone of flies and a confounding stench of dead flesh, old and new, baffled her

Tarchia
ankylosaur
ornithischian
herbivore
12 ft.
1500 lbs.
(adult size)
Upper Cretaceous
Mongolia:
arid semi-desert

senses. She could not see the source of it all. She drove herself on ahead. She stopped again, near bones. A grossly thickened skull, the rubble of forelegs, the odd stumpy digits fallen into the tray of shoulderbone, the broken low scaffold of ribs conveyed nothing . . . or not enough. She went slowly ahead, tromped over thick bones and scattered fragments of pelvis and along the broken articulation of tailbones, until at the end, she came to the great bony mace like her own, like that of all her kind. She paused, listened, sniffed—and froze. She gave out a horrific snort. One ankylosaur from the back of the herd, squealing, lumbered in fright through the others and toward her. She stopped the offender with a swing of her tail and offered her great blunt bite. Her consort chased the skittish one back to the rear.

Where they were, the strict construction of the defile had collapsed in on itself. On one side, the strew of bones under the cycloning flies gave way to an easy rise. A thick soft sapling forest beckoned from the soil among the rocks, the leaves and fronds tossing green light all about. The other wall of the defile cut barrenly away in the other direction. The troop milled about until, from the scarp just adjacent, an accumulating bleat of terror rushed down toward them. A small blot dove, hit rock, elongated, hit rock, broke, hit again, broke the other way and, tumbling end over end over end, flew into space to smash earth in front of the herd. Shattered, on its back, the thescelosaur kicked into the air. It plunged its claws into empty air. Dying or dead, it snapped its beak on air. The details of its destruction—eye hanging on nerve from socket, loops of entrails—conveyed nothing to the ancient female, but the smell of fresh blood did. She twisted her body, hurled herself past the dead animal and with something like speed continued on her way down the barren defile.

Most of the troop automatically followed her. A small number in distraction made their way up the green sappy rise, chomping and foraging avidly for a short while. Then they heard the pack of carnosaurs, who had frightened the thescelosaur over the edge of the crevice, and who now were stalking downhill to divide its flesh. In the sudden convergence and disarray, the first sweep of a clubbed tail shattered the ankle of an

unwary carnosaur. The rest of the pack attacked. The ankylosaurs struggled toward each other to regroup. Some were singled out by pairs of hunters, a few managed to break away. Waddling and lunging, they set out on the path taken by the ancient female, her consort and the rest of the troop, who now were working their way on down the other wall of the defile to where the terrain was beginning to open ahead of them again.

FEATHERS

Three small, skin-winged pterosaurs cut fancy circles around archaeopteryx's descent. Their harassment is brief because archaeopteryx soon hits ground. The pterosaurs keep circling because something about the landing suggests archaeopteryx might have killed himself, but he quickly springs up and races off.

Archaeopteryx lives very close to the edge. He stalks through sedge and bracken, putting the feathers on his forelegs to good use flushing out crickets and grasshoppers.

Sometimes he comes up with nothing more than a few seeds or a flying ant. Fleeing some hungry, unfeathered close relative down a long hill, archaeopteryx might amaze his pursuer by feathering out and kicking off into the air across gullies and washes. The acute turns at full speed and the high flapping leaps sometimes work for archaeopteryx and sometimes not. Escaping or chasing, archaeopteryx finds feathers about as much a hindrance as a help.

Night falls, this one chillier than any other in recent times. The mist thickens to a drizzle and when it gets colder, the drizzle turns to rain. There is enough light for archaeopteryx to find a tree, but he has to climb almost entirely by feel—awkwardly, slowly, the little claws at the joints of his

Archaeopteryx was a small animal. Fortunately it did not have to deal with voracious lizards like these in the Jurassic. If its Cretaceous descendants had stayed on the ground, this was a situation they might have faced—reason enough to take the air! Not only did flight open up new feeding opportunities, it was also an effective means of keeping out of harm's way.
—P.D.

folded wings scrabbling to secure every step upwards. Teetering just slightly, archaeopteryx perches where branch joins trunk and tucks his head under his wing.

Below, with their feet in cold muck, prey and predator, great and small, steam faintly for a while. As their skins chill, the steaming stops. They move for warmth, huddle for warmth.

Threading in rivulets down pebbled hides, sheeting over plates, knobs, and spikes, the rain races also in unbroken drops down feathers to the ground below. Archaeopteryx sleeps warm.

After the cold night, the short day dawns cold and foul. Archaeopteryx stretches head and neck straight up, stretches feathered arms out wide. Snaking his head

this way and that, he seeks an easy way down out of the tree. About to back down from branch to twig to branch, on impulse archaeopteryx suddenly dives through the thicket of leaves. Elbowing apart sticks and greenery, he finds open air in which to spread wings and glide to the ground. A cloud of dying leaves sifts down about him. Archaeopteryx gets to his feet, rattles out some kind of announcement to the leaden skies and paces springily away to find food, which he quickly does.

Camptosaurs were attending clutches of their eggs. Too cold and sick to go for archaeopteryx, they watch, or do not watch, as he pecks open the eggs and gobbles up yolks and soft embryos. Later, after battening on insects whose numbers are exploding

Above:

Archaeopteryx
archaeornithid
avian
insectivore
1 ft.
1 lb.
Upper Jurassic
Germany:
forest, plain
adjacent to lagoon

On the next page,
top to bottom:

Longisquama
theocodont
archosaur
insectivore
12 inches
4 ounces
Middle Triassic
swamps
Turkestan, Russia

Icarosaurus
squamatan
lepidosaur
insectivore
12 inches
4 ounces
Upper Triassic
New Jersey
lake-edge swamps

from the carcasses everywhere about, archaeopteryx improves the level of his diet: lizards and tiny soft turtles and great spiders and the rapid—not rapid enough—small furred animals which feed on the insects. . . .

Never satisfied, archaeopteryx yearns for it all: earthworms, carrion, rove beetles and gnats, great dragonflies, even the fish of lakes and seas, seeds of weed, fruit of podocarpus, and the harvest atop the tallest trees. Straining weak wings toward his goals, archaeopteryx hops high and glides long, but never crosses the threshold of great success. It will be left to his own triumphantly winging progeny, the birds, to achieve everything archaeopteryx has yearned for.

GLIDER

Just hatched, the young icarosaur must dodge almost every creature slightly larger than himself as he seeks out aphid, beetle, and fly. Save for his ruby pinpoint eye, he looks like any other tiny lizard until, some days older, he shows a flattening of ribcage. The fine bones extend to the sides. At first, they make no difference, then they slow him down. In that span of time, a great number of his brood are nipped by larger lizards, even by turtles. He survives. The fine bones, webbed with translucent skin, extend. He hops through air to land one body length or two beyond where his pursuer or prey might expect.

The mixed stand of cycads, ginkgo and club moss is interlaced not by the boughs of these trees, but by the leaps and glides of the icarosaur and his kind. He cleans a cycad of grubs and small insects. His leap from the top of the tree carries him not in a soft tumbling fall to its base, but flat to the bottom of another, on which he begins to climb again. The distance along the ground between boles is a distance icarosaur does not often have to walk.

TREES

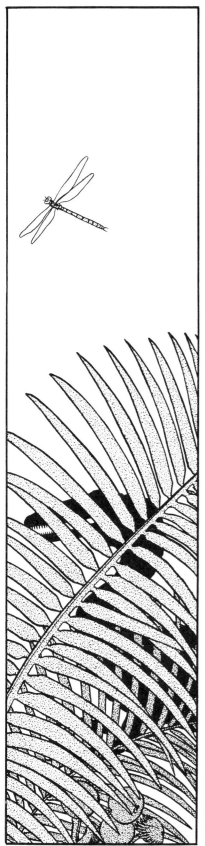

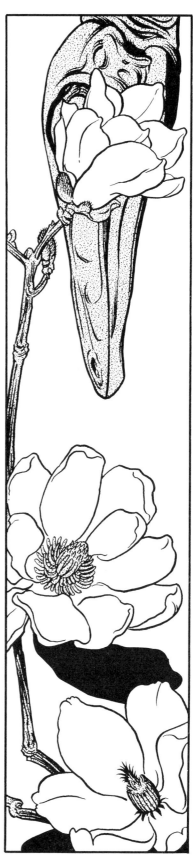

Far left, top:

Protolindenia

Bottom:

Procompsagnathus
Triassic
Tree:
Cycad

Center:

Gnathosaurus
Jurassic
Tree:
Redwood

Left:

Dromiceiomimus
Cretaceous
Tree:
Magnolia

FLOWERS

I n the benign climate, it was not necessary to migrate with the sun; instead, the herd tended to flow with the tides of green which the rainy season fostered. The mild chills did not bother them as long as vegetation thrived. But then one solstice brought bitter wind and cold nights. In disarray, the herd scattered, each animal walking day and night to fight off the final cold. Some fell from exhaustion. Others wandered into winter, and then fell. The survivors wandered in pursuit of the capricious warm weather.

From another region, the bird flocks had brought and scattered seeds of new vegetation. These sprouted and climbed sunward, leaving in competition lifeless shade. Their roots sucked the ground dry. The migrating herd stumbled into slow collision with the billowing progress of the flowering plants. They chewed hard on the tough, succulent leaves. Harvesting the blooms, they stirred up clouds of the new pollen.

The season progressed. The herd breasted the waves of colors, smells, textures, tastes and flower dust which they had never encountered before. They consumed much of it and pushed on through. In this same season, they found a second wave. Luxuriating in the fragrant growth, they began to choke: deep, almost endless hacking coughs, bubbles of mucus at the nostrils, inflamed eyes, running tears. They wiped their muzzles and cheeks hard against the ground. First one, then others experienced a serpentine recoil of the neck, a violent expulsion of mucus, pollen, saliva, and air: a sneeze which blasted flowers from their stems.

With time, the herd became inured to the side effects of the new growth: they plundered through, crunching seeds, nuts, pits, and slobbering sweet berries.

Opposite:

Leptoceratops
*ceratopsian
ornithischian
herbivore
5-8 ft.
100-200 lbs.
Upper Cretaceous
Alberta, Wyoming:
wet floodplains
swamp forests*

*Leptoceratops is a primitive horned dinosaur. It resembles its cousin, the famous Protoceratops of Mongolia, in both size and shape, but is even more primitive. For instance, its bony frill at the back of the head is even smaller than Protoceratop's. An animal like Leptoceratops was the ancestor of mighty Triceratops, but it lived in the time of Triceratops itself!
—P.D.*

MAMMALS

he top of the tree, the hole in the ground, and night: their domain. Some eat insects and fill in with buds and seeds, others eat buds and seeds and fill in with insects. An occasional lizard is taken.

Perhaps the largest used to venture forth at night to raid nests and to drag hatchlings back to their small lairs. The dinosaurs began to tend their nests and guard their young. Mammals retreated, and would continue to retreat. Most footprints will soon belong to dinosaurs, which no mammal will dare follow, or even crouch to hide in.

Now, on the ground, and only for the time being, whether down from a tree or out of a brake or up from a hole, all kinds of mammals move rapidly and rehearse their terrain again and again. They are not easy to catch. Agile and quick to bite, they are not easy to kill. Only a few kinds of pterosaur share with them that almost singular feature, fur. The pterosaurs are easier to kill but harder to catch. Some carnosaurs, having devoured one or the other, simply pass through and evacuate the small bones and hair; others cough up the remains in pellets.

Listening . . . the tiny curve of ear outside the skull and extra devices inside give the mammal a little more acuity than the dinosaur has. Watching . . . until the light fades, the great size and refinement of most saurian eyes give them superior sight by day, whereafter the reflecting layer and special grain of the mammal's eye give the advantage. Smelling . . . yielding in acuity only to moths and some fishes, and in that only for

specific substances, the mammalian nose is far the best in general usefulness, except, in latter days, by the unparalleled olfactory apparatus of the hadrosaurs, who fortunately have no interest in mammals.

In the course of recent events, the dinosaurs have posed no great threat to the mammals. The entire archosaurian hegemony is such, however, that the mammals are kept stringently to their obscure place. The great constraint on their line is not that of food supply—even though some have to creep forth to pick apart carnosaur droppings for the bits of bone and gristle—but space. The mammals may not take to the air, swim more than a few strokes, nor even inhabit good level ground. They are interdicted from growth itself. Burrowing under carcasses for swarms of insect life and meat, munching green shoots and wrestling newts and earthworms to death, the mammals could disappear from earth without significant effect on any line of archosaurs.

The mammals have always tended their young somewhat more closely than the dinosaurs have. The late development of pouches and of milk glands has lengthened the term of that care with the result that mammalian young move out into their world—constricted though it may be—well equipped to exploit its resources and to escape its dangers. Their new security, however, is challenged by a new type of dinosaur: speeding on long hind legs, guided by the largest, sharpest eyes which exist, sharp of tooth and quick of hand. These hunters relentlessly track the fleeing mammals through each twist and turn, no matter how

Opposite:

Brachiosaurus
sauropod
saurischian
herbivore
70 ft.
40 tons
Upper Jurassic
Colorado Tanzania:
wet and dry
floodplains

often rehearsed. The new dinosaurs, just a season or two out of the egg, are especially devastating as they drive their prey through the closest thickets and even partially up trees or lie in wait for them at the mouths of their burrows. Plainly, the domain of the entire mammalian line, worldwide, will be reduced to an insignificant toehold in the environs, barring some improbable major cataclysm.

INSECTS

Opposite:

Ornitholestes
coelurosaur
saurischian
carnivore,
insectivore
6 ft.
40-70 lbs.
Upper Jurassic
Wyoming:
floodplain,
riverbank

*Insects are actual
size.*

Right:

A. Notocupes
lapidarius
(Cupedidae)
B. Protoscelis
jurassica
(Chrysomelidae)
C. Monstrocoreus
quadrimaculatus
D. Archodromus
comptus
(Staphylinidae)
E. Miridoides
mesozoicus
(Miridae)
F. Globoides
oculatus
(Staphylinidae)
G. Archegetes
neuropterorum
H. Conocephalopsis
capito
I. Tersus
crassicornis
J. Cyrtophyllites
rogeri
K. Psuedosirex
(Psuedosiricidae)
L. Mesopsychopsis
hospes
M. Aeschnidium
densum
N. Ensiferorum
propingua
(Ensifera)

A hundred million years ago, thirty inch dragonflies droned over foot-long cockroaches. Insects flew with abandon long before any animal with a backbone dared attempt the feat. When finally the sky was swept by pterosaurs and birds, they could be viewed as late arrivals. Mayflies, beetles, bugs, grasshoppers, midges, in

fact, two-thirds of all orders of living insects were represented in the Mesozoic Era.

If any group has no business to be found in the fossil record, surely it is the insects. They have no bones, no truly hard parts, only protein-rich, biodegradable chitinous exoskeletons. Yet at certain times and in certain places these six-legged creatures obliged. Dragonflies and cockroaches tumbled into three hundred million year old swamp deposits in Europe, flies and mosquitoes rained down into lovely, fine-grained lake sediments a few tens of millions of years old in Colorado and Wyoming. Best of all, golden tears of resin, wept by Baltic pines fifty million years ago, locked into amber perfect specimens of ants, fleas, lice and mites.

But such events are rare and the record of insects is woeful: Cretaceous butterflies are known from a single chunk of a single specimen; Cretaceous ants have only recently been recorded. We must patiently wait while the earth yields up treasures from the Age of Reptiles.

When new finds are made, they will not take us completely by surprise. Insects did not evolve in a biological vacuum. Insects and flowers today enjoy exquisite, mutually beneficial relationships. Flowering plants appeared in the Lower Cretaceous, some 100 million years ago, and offered new opportunities for insects to evolve.

COOL WEATHER

Camptosaurus
ornithopod
ornithischian
herbivore

3 ft. - 17 ft.
20 lbs. - 2000 lbs.
Upper Jurassic
Wyoming, Colorado,

Utah, England:
wet and dry
floodplains

COLD WEATHER

Iguanodon
ornithopod
ornithischian
herbivore
15-30 ft.
1-6 tons
Lower Cretaceous
England, Belgium:
swamps beside large
lake complex

The following paint-
ing on the right
shows the position
of stars of the Big
Dipper as they may
have appeared dur-
ing the Cretaceous
Period.

To stay with the warmth, all save one iguanadon followed the retreat and return of the sun, which sufficed until such time as the herd found themselves blocked by an arm of the new sea. When the warmth slid by them and away out over the water, all were left to die of the cold except that one and those who, swimming out as if to cross a familiar marsh, drowned or went down in the jaws of sea creatures.

Laden with eggs, that single iguanadon was guided by the configuration three fading stars made with the moonset. For many seasons there had been no great difference between her course and that of the others. Now they diverged. She angled off from the doomed herd to traverse a deepening winter. At first she nosed through rime for wilted greenery, then soon was gouging with thumb spikes down into plates of congealed snow. When the snow deepened, she kicked talons through it for the meager vegetation underneath, shaving the green from the frozen surface until dirt came up in her mouth. She then moved on.

When the bone-thin moon and the configuration of stars could not be seen, she meandered without straying far from her path. To sleep or rest meant never to move again. She ate whatever dead growth bristled above the snow. Marching on numb feet along the course the remote bits of light dictated, she became a wraith of two fixed eyes set within jutting bones. In the snow, soft blue, or hard blinding white, or smeared with orange, there was not a single track. She ate twigs, stripped the bark of dead trees, and progressed until the snow thinned to a shell of dripping ice. Almost without appetite, she sluggishly crunched the frozen water up along with the pallid greenery underneath, and evacuated watery streams which burned down along her haunches.

The course of stars and moon took her through days less cold, a few colder, then warmer and on into increasing warmth, green growth, and her own strength. When those combined correctly in a fervent landscape for the while empty of opposing life, she hastily scratched out a suggestion of a nest, and dropped into it egg after egg after egg.

WARM WEATHER

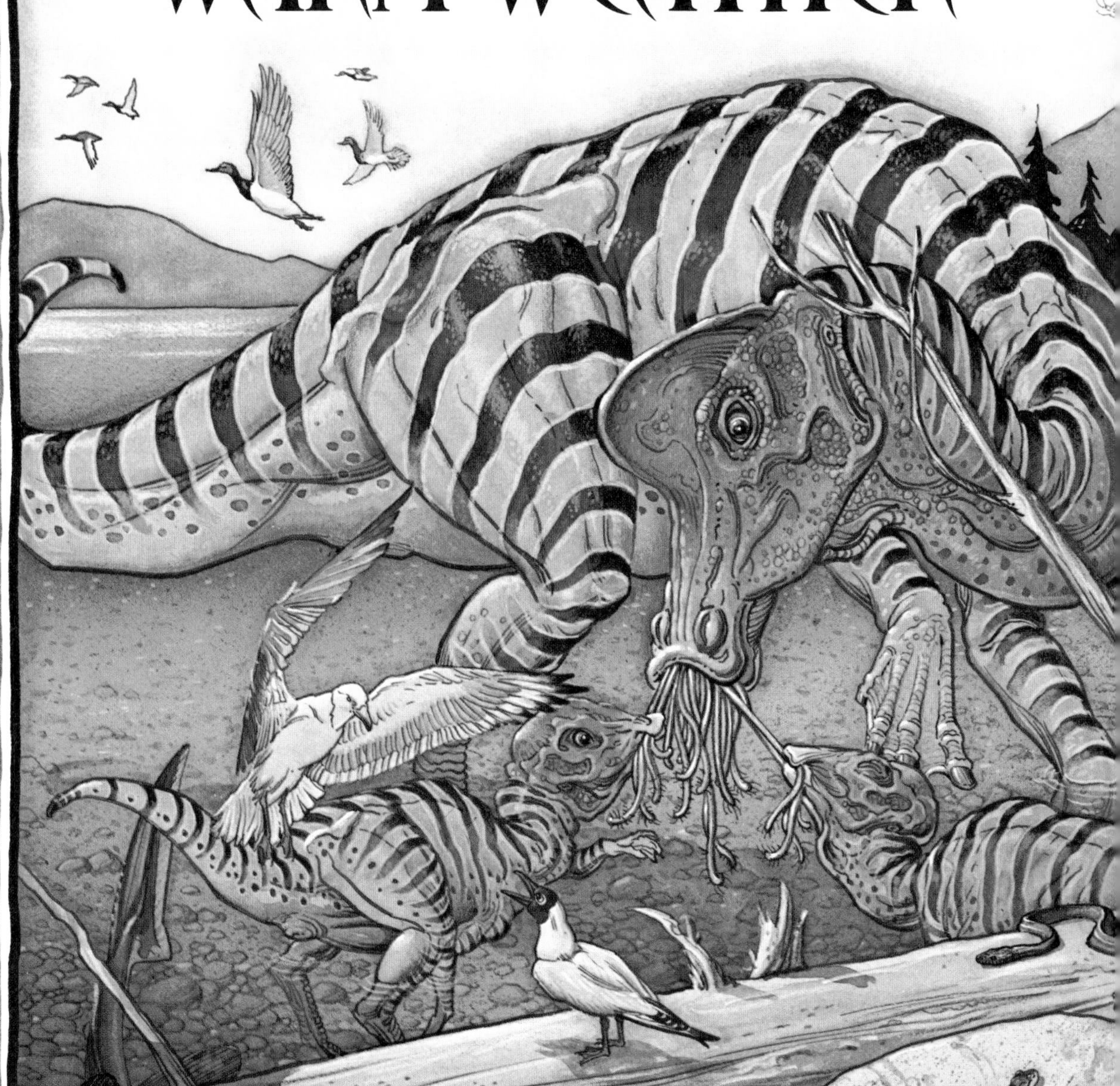

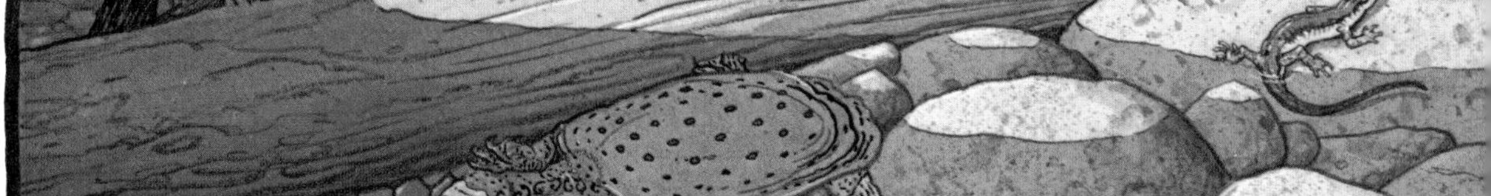

Corythosaurus
hadrosaur
ornithischian
herbivore
10-30 ft.
400 lbs-3 tons
Upper Cretaceous
Alberta:
floodplains,
lakes, rivers,
swamp (i.e., in
and out of water)

All of the animals
in this Cretaceous
Period scene also
exist today, except
the members of the
hadrosaur species,
Corythosaurus.
These animals
include: ducks,
heron, dragonfly,
terns, opossum,
frogs, gulls, flamin-
gos, plovers, snails,
lizard, tortoise, tur-
tles, snake, gar,
sturgeon, salaman-
der, water beetle,
crocodile, bowfin
and loon.

HOT WEATHER

I t was hotter than hot, drier than bones, and the sun was not even high. There could be no place worse than where he was, so the ankylosaur kept walking, for aside from the four or five scrambling lunges he could make in time of trouble, walking was the only gait he had.

In such heat, it would have been better to be the size of the lizards which skittered all around him. *They* could shade themselves under a twig and cool off. Or to be the size of the small furry animals which burrowed under the clumps of dryland weed and grass down to the cool. But the ankylosaur was too thirsty, and the vegetation these minute creatures inhabited too dry, for him even to take a bite. There was nothing to do but keep on walking.

It would have been good to have the lean, light build and long hind legs of struthiomimus, who looked like an enormous, unfeathered, stretched out bird. A few of this sort skipped obliviously by, staying only to scare up and eat some lizards, crop dry sedge, and crunch seed pods still on a vetch vine. They seemed to enjoy eating food like that. Even so, they soon sped off to greener pastures, and were out of sight by the time the ankylosaur had gone ten times the length of his body.

Since there was no way for him to become lean and swift like struthiomimus, the ability to sweat would have been the ankylosaur's salvation. But he knew nothing about sweat. Dragging his heavy clubbed tail, he walked into the high scattered shade of an acacia tree. Nothing to do there but rest and walk on out again.

Resuming his course, pressing one heavy print in the loose, sandy earth, and then another, the ankylosaur did not appreciate the lifesaving durability of his armor, only its

weight, and saw his club only as something that had to be dragged over the hot earth. He opened his mouth wide to pant. It was a refined mouth, accustomed to the better things in life. With it he sorted out the few poisonous fungi from the good ones, and enjoyed fallen fruit, carrion, tubers, berries, sprouted nuts, and the bitesome green balled fists of ferns just up. Now he was parching his mouth on hot dry air. It was a fine point whether he could afford to spend his body's water for the cooling effect; he just let his body make the decisions as he went along.

Lacking the special skills to combat the heat, and being big, bulky, slow, and now dangerously overheated, he knew he had to find the best and last resort, water. His horny feet were hot, but he kept moving them. The terrain began to slope downward, not enough to help his progress much but not a hindrance either. Inside, he was as tough as his armor.

Finally he stopped in something like perplexity. He had gained the shore of a lake he remembered, but what was under his feet was mud baked into wafers with the edges curled up. Where another creature might have expired on the spot, the ankylosaur marched straight ahead. His eyesight, none too keen beyond ten body lengths, was registering something in the distant blur of light. He made for that as fast as he could . . . .

It was no longer a lake, not even a pond, but it was not merely mud either; there was water in it. The ankylosaur did not scramble, nor lunge, but continued to proceed straight ahead to the cool. Then he sank his head and, straining out the grosser junk with his teeth, sucked in copiously. After lifting his head for air, he drank more and then wallowed his whole length and breadth into the ooze, vocalizing for the first time that day, and loudly.

Ankylosaurus
ankylosaur
ornithischian
herbivore
15 ft.
3 tons
Upper Cretaceous
Alberta, Mongolia:
lowland swamp,
riverbank

DISEASE

The herd of ceratopsians stumbled on, but their numbers had been badly depleted. Surprisingly, some yearlings and two-year-olds still remained among the tattered assemblage. Faces were gaunt, limb muscles shriveled, ribs conspicuous. The fiery orange colors that had once decorated the proud head-shields of the large males had dulled to umber. The sun glared down on the withered landscape. In an area that had been blessed by generous rainfall and lush vegetation, such a merciless drought hadn't been seen in a thousand years.

Movement was painfully slow. For weeks, fodder had been inadequate both in quality and in quantity, becoming increasingly fibrous and poorer in protein, vitamins and minerals. It had been ten days since there had been food of any description. The ceratopsian's wasted bodies were racked with a variety of afflictions they no longer had the strength to resist. In some, vitamin deficiencies wrought a cruel toll. Gums bled, eyes were dimmed with pus, eyelids were badly puffed. They gasped and wheezed for breath with open mouths and dripping noses. Others in the band showed a reptilian sort of mange—spreading patches of dead and dying skin on the flanks, limbs and tail, caused by a virulent fungus. The resulting lesions in the thick hide opened avenues for invasion of the body by other disease-causing agents: flies laid their eggs and the white maggots wriggled.

Inside the hapless beasts, throats, stomachs and guts were ravaged by the fungus as well. The lead male showed none of the external signs that most of his charges presented, yet he too moved slowly, painfully, dazedly. He had passed bloody stools that were hallmarks of a virulent infectious amoeba of the gut. He laboriously surmounted the bank of what had formerly been a moderate-sized watercourse, swung his head back to survey his straggling troup, then lurched and with a tragic moan tumbled unwillingly into the dry channel bottom. He moved no more.

Now leaderless, the feeble ceratopsians were in a state of confusion. In normal times, they had dispersed throughout the verdant plain and saw others of their kind only casually. But in this time of crisis they had all come together in search for food and water. Too far gone to regroup, they milled about the fallen body aimlessly, trampling his tail and legs, and cracking his bones underfoot. None left the site, and within two days all were dead. Decay, putrefaction, scattering and bleaching worked their deteriorating processes on the ceratopsians.

Two years later the rains returned, the landscape was clothed again in green, the river bubbled in its channel. The bare bones of the fallen ceratopsians shuddered under the impact of the waterflow, moved short distances downstream, or oriented themselves so as to minimize the push of the current, and were buried and forgotten. Soon, ceratopsians were cavorting in the surroundings once again, immigrants from regions that had not been ravaged by drought.

Triceratops
ceratopsian
ornithischian
herbivore
20-30 ft.
4-6 tons
Upper Cretaceous
Wyoming, Montana, Alberta:
floodplains,
swamp forests

DEATH

Haplocanthosaurus
sauropod
saurischian
herbivore
30-50 ft.
5-10 tons
Upper Jurassic
Colorado:
floodplains,
riverbanks, swamps

Ceratosaurus
carnosaur
saurischian
carnivore scavenger
15-20 ft.
1-2 tons
Upper Jurassic
Wyoming,
Colorado, Utah:
floodplains,
river and lake
shores

The carnosaur swung his weight on a hind leg not much more flexible than a tree stump. Broken at knee and ankle, the joints of the leg had long ago almost fused. Opposite him, a sauropod backed off. Showing scars on her neck and flanks where the same carnosaur, that same long time ago, had dragged her from the protection of her herd and had almost torn the life from her, she bore even deeper scars in her patterns of defense. She now shied from every clash with the carnosaur's jaws and reared back on her hind legs away from every offering of his curved horn.

She had saved herself long ago by wheeling and thrashing about until the earth-shaking tread of the rest of her herd had overrun, then crushed, the carnosaur's leg into the ground. This time however, the herd was scattered, was blank to her peril. Avoiding his charge at her shoulder, she backed toward the edge.

The carnosaur thrust his bad leg forward, lurched on it, strode with the good one and braced himself directly in front of the other to deliver a roaring hiss like steam from split rock. The sauropod bolted to one side and was almost past the carnosaur when a slash of his horn up into empty air set her rearing again. Before he was down on all fours, the carnosaur positioned himself again in front of her.

It was as if the sauropod's wounds, those which had streamed blood for days and had become infected and maggot-blown long after that, were still open. The sauropod stepped back until one great foot, placed in empty air, had to come forward again. Bracing himself, the carnosaur pivoted stiffly from one side to the other, chomped empty jaws, and himself reared up. The sauropod cringed back: her head, recoiled on the long supple neck, took in the emptiness of the air behind her, and something of the fall, the long fall. Pebbles, rocks, then a boulder crumbled over the precipice, and were not heard to strike earth. The carnosaur lunged in, almost to engage his prey, who again hoisted forelegs high, though not to strike back. As she again came down, enough of the cliff's rim broke to drop one hind leg and then the other over the edge. The sauropod surged on her front two, tore belly hide along broken stone, pitched and yawed to her feet and, without registering the significance of her action, shouldered the carnosaur aside as she regained solid ground.

Recovering his balance, the carnosaur attacked with a thrust of his horn, missed, dodged a sweep of the sauropod's massive tail, and repositioned himself. The sauropod again backed to the edge, and, this time, when the carnosaur lunged in the direction of her neck, she fell, and fell, and could be heard to hit ground.

The carnosaur craned over the edge to locate his prey, then hobbled along to find a way down the chasm. It was ingrained in him that should he lose sight of the spoils for more than a few moments, the location and even the fact of the kill would be entirely lost to him. Periodically, therefore, he would stop to extend his dire head over the edge, so as to keep himself oriented to the dead animal far below.

SCAVENGERS

The big animal had lived long enough to see the shoots and sprouts whose tops he had chewed long ago grow up to become an airy pasture largely out of reach, the boles of which being far too stout to bend down. Progenitor of generation after generation of chewers of seeds and fronds, he extended himself finally out upon earth, dying, not of any carnosaur's bite or slash, but of a long inhabitation of small beings which, cruising the vessels of his body, finally overwhelmed the capacity of the organs which cleansed his blood. Some of the rest of the herd, moving past, stopped to lean down, sense the situation and nudge him. He was dead close to the instant when the first of the meat-eaters would find him, sink teeth into his neck.

Only the largest of these had teeth long enough to get through the skin of even the underbelly: Tarbosaur dug talons in, clamped jaws, heaved mightily up and back, and left only slashes. Changing angles of bite, tarbosaur tore again and again, his slashes criss-crossing slashes until finally the body yielded shreds, then chunks.

Arriving in chaotic order, scavengers. Coelurosaurs dashed in and out, took nips. Flies whizzed in for the blood, studding the carcass with green, gold, blue: they were timed to feed only, and not yet lay eggs, for those would have been eaten up with the torn meat. Under the carcass, death-watch and rove beetles tunnelling in the bounty multiplied, for the time safe from the lizards already climbing the flesh and arched staves of bones above. Various tides of mold and rot contended with one another, and soon repelled the tarbosaur, who, taking one last bite, swallowed the cysts of the minute beings which had helped bring the big animal down, and so completed their cycle into another generation. Next, the other scavengers quit the festering cadaver, leaving it to wave after wave of insects and their larvae to take on down, until its framework of bones rose bare. To the bones, an enormous tortoise, ever needful of minerals, came periodically to grind down in his great beak.

Saurolophus
hadrosaur
ornithischian
herbivore
25-40 ft.
3-6 tons
Upper Cretaceous
Alberta, Mongolia:
floodplain, swamp
forest, river, lake

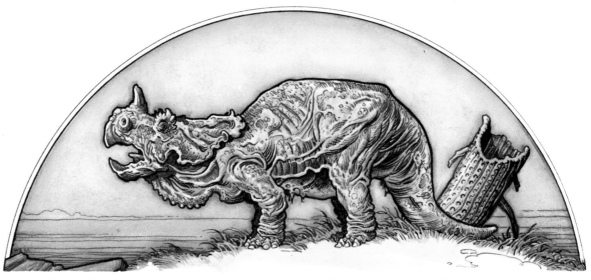

THE LIFE CYCLE OF CENTROSAURUS

L eaning hard, the two animals ground abrasively against each other. The older did so many times a day, whether his flanks were being tormented by huge biting flies or not. The two went back to enjoy vegetation so tender it scarcely had to be chewed. The dozen or so centrosaurs, having drifted into a sweep of forest which had burned down to stumps, were eagerly using their beaks on such growth as root sprouts, fungi shaped in knobs and loaves and shelves and fans, fruited brambles, and the sudden vines which follow fire.

The oldest of the herd, the spines of whose deeply scarred escutcheon had healed crookedly, would occasionally stop browsing, stop chewing, and simply stand. And then resume. He scraped some charcoal off a fallen log, licked out a pocket of tasty ash under a branch, then levered the bole up and away with his horn. The depression was lined with blanched roots and was swarming with the creatures which live under logs. He cleaned the length of the trough down to brown earth, then turned to more usual forage. Soon he felt the need for another hide scraping. He swung his massive head to locate a likely partner. His eyes were so clouded by cataracts that he had to wait until one moved. . . .

His horn was just long enough to pip through the shell. He was so small an adult foot would have flattened him, and so unlike an adult in form that neither parent would have hesitated to do so. A struthiomimus attending the hatching was occupied with the remains of a sibling and did not go after him. Blind to details, centrosaurus reacted to the pattern of large movement and scrambled rapidly off into the thicket. He was to live there for a year in comparative safety, leaving it only when drawn by the soft amber radiance of fallen persimmons or by the luminescence of a carcass at night. Time and again some looming bulk would send him off on two churning hind legs until the thicket brought him to all fours again. Growing rapidly on the abundant mixed

diet, he entered a phase not many of his kind survived. Now exclusively quadruped, he was too heavy to run, not heavy enough to fight. Grown too big for the thicket, he was not big enough for the forest. Too grown to round out his menu with grubs and salamanders, he was not grown enough to range and rip down the copious vegetations he needed to keep growing.

He needed to join a herd, and found a large one, but the herd was troubled by some sense of its own numbers: the females drove him away. While still in sight of them, he was set upon by the carnosaur which had been trailing the herd for days. Easily straddling the desperate upward thrusts of the young centrosaur and stepping away from his bites, the carnosaur harried him to the ground, then hoisted him upright in jaws clamped into the shield of his nape. Centrosaur arched, his horn hit not air, not bony ridge, not jaw, but the eye. The horrific shake which the carnosaur gave him drove the horn deeper, and then through the base of the orbit. The carnosaur let go, and lurched away. The herd, which would have defended one of its own, was gone.

Centrosaurus
ceratopsian
ornithischian
herbivore
5 - 20 ft.
50 lbs - 3 tons
Upper Cretaceous
Alberta:
lowland forest,
swamp, floodplain

Centrosaur wandered. His wounds gradually healed, but he could not get enough of the good forage he needed for

growth. He survived on dry sedge, vetch, briar, bark. . . . When finally he discovered and approached a small herd of his kind, he was so emaciated that his ribs showed through the thick horny hide. The herd accepted him without challenge or welcome. Now he could share in the harvest of a downed tree, drink water in safety, lay claim to groves, and, before many seasons had gone by, leave the huddle of juveniles and egg-heavy females to join in the defense of the herd. Not as belligerent as some other ceratopians, the centrosaurs would gather, face a predator, and wait. If the predator did not retreat, the more aggressive among the centrosaurs would charge ahead, then stop. Those behind would catch up and trundle on ahead, and then stop. The first group would repeat this process. The final outcome was left up to the predator.

Centrosaur aged. Duels were won and lost, and won again; and matings were performed with their long stylized courtships and brief spasmodic couplings. The herd returned to a mature forest: centrosaur's old thicket. He quit duels, unenraged, after a few ritual hits with the horns and a few shoves. He coupled with females as available. . . .

Centrosaur jerked his head up at the sound of a barrage of warning grunts. The member of the herd nearest to the apparition was the last to see it. Four huge male centrosaurs lumbered by and stopped; four more behind them. They were preparing for a skirmish— it set centrosaur's blood and juices flowing as nothing else, and their heat unstiffened his joints. Everything was in motion, he could see to take his part with no difficulty. Firing off staccato grunts, he charged ahead, then stopped. He saw others in turn thunder on by. In the general direction of wherever and whatever the adversary might be, he charged ahead again.

DINOSAUR DIMENSIONS

by Dr. Peter Dodson

SMALLEST

T he smallest known dinosaurs are babies—mere hatchlings. This is a truism, so there's no surprise in that. However, it is eye opening that the smallest, presumably adult dinosaur known was only about two feet long: *Compsognathus,* from the Upper Jurassic Period of Gemany. What is truly surprising is that the very smallest dinosaur of which we have a record is a hatchling that would have been literally knee-high to a pigeon! *Psittacosaurus* was a Cretaceous dinosaur from Mongolia that would have attained the stunning adult length of about four and one-half feet, based on largest known specimens. The smallest is a skull that measures barely an inch long; placed on a quarter, it would barely overhang the edge. The length of this animal would have been about nine inches. Yet this animal was not just out of the egg. It had already tasted the fruits of the earth, for its teeth already show wear produced only by use!

Psittacosaurs were small, three-toed bipeds which were thinking about becoming horned dinosaurs. That is, they seem to represent a structural stage through which horned dinosaurs passed; though they lacked horns and a frill, they had the very characteristic beak of horned dinosaurs. Mongolia seems to be a happy hunting ground for very small dinosaurs; at least five different kinds of six-foot or smaller adults have been found there.

Probably the next smallest baby dinosaur specimen is that of a Triassic prosauropod, *Mussaurus,* from South America, whose skull measures an inch and a quarter long, the entire animal having been only twelve or thirteen inches long.

The nearly three foot long baby hadrosaurs found in a single nest in Montana were giants by comparison. Like the baby *Psittacosaurus,* the teeth of these babies show wear, indicating that they had been feeding on tough foodstuffs for several months already. The fact that the fifteen nestlings were still together some months after hatching suggests that their mother, whose skull was found nearby, may have cared for them; hence the name *Maiasaura,* meaning "good mother lizard."

Psittacosaurus
ornithopod
ornithischian
herbivore
9 inches-5 ft.
6 oz.-40 lbs.
Upper Cretaceous
Mongolia:
dry semi-desert

TALLEST

The desire of paleontologists to speculate on the sizes of dinosaurs is simply irresistible—we cannot help ourselves. It is perhaps lamentable that we must almost always estimate, for it is a simple fact of paleontological life that the skeletons of dinosaurs are almost never found complete. This is especially true of the very large dinosaurs, the sauropods. It is probably correct to suggest that the larger the dinosaur, the less likely the chance of finding it complete.

When an animal dies, its lifeless components are in disequilibrium with its surroundings. All sorts of interesting processes work to reduce muscles, nerves, vessels, organs and sinues to the simple compounds from which they were synthesized in life. Whether mighty predator or lowly worm, the agents of decomposition will result in bone being separated from bone and reduced to powder to ultimately disappear without trace. These inexorable destructive processes are arrested if a carcass is draped in entombing sediment. Animals that die in a silt-choken stream have a much greater chance of prompt burial with relatively little loss of body parts than do animals that breathe their last on a parched, sun-drenched plain.

The second chance for bones to be shattered, fragmented, and lost comes when the earth yields up her treasures to the wondering eyes of the paleontologist. Erosion, by howling wind and running water, is the force by which skeletons are freed from the rock that encloses them, but this same process wreaks havoc on the exposed, fossilized bones before many years have passed.

How are skeletons discovered? How does the bone hunter know where to dig? One does not dig at a blank spot in hopes that bones will be found there; rather, one hones in on a tell-tale trail of fragments cascading down a hillside. Erosion has begun her work, and the paleontologist takes over—hopefully not too late.

Without glue and plaster there would be no paleontology. Although few dinosaurs have ever been found truly complete, there is much accomplished through paleontologi-cal research and ingenuity. We find a head and neck of one specimen, the trunk and tail of another, the trunk and neck of a third. Pretty soon, we have a clear idea of what the animal looked like and how big it was. The largest dinosaurs were certainly the sauropods: Brontosaurus (or as it is known scientifically, Apatosaurus) and his friends. Even if we knew nothing of the backbones of these animals, we would still be certain of this—for what else can one conclude of an animal whose forearm was seven feet long? Sauropods not only had long legs but long necks as well. The best reason to have a long neck, as giraffe-watchers know, is to reach high up into trees to browse on luxuriant fodder that other animals cannot reach. However, the long neck of a giraffe and the long neck of a sauropod are two different things. A very large giraffe could barely reach nineteen feet off the ground. Among sauropods, a fifteen-foot neck starting from a platform of ten feet off the ground was strictly routine. In fact, some scientists believe that Brontosaurus, using its long, heavy tail as a counterbalance, actually reared up on its hindlegs and, with its otherwise hard-to-explain short forelegs resting on the trunk of a tree, reached up to heights of thirty or thirty-five feet to browse on tasty tree-top vegetation. Its cousin, Brachiosaurus, didn't even strain to reach forty feet. His tail was short, his trunk long; no standing on hindlegs for him. But he differed from all his cousins in that his front legs were longer than his hind. His shoulder was thirteen feet off the ground; his ribs were nine feet long. He stood nineteen feet tall; the tallest giraffe could not even peer over the back of his neck! And what a neck it was, full, luxuriant twenty-nine feet long, affording a reach that probably exceeded forty feet.

Was Brachiosaurus the tallest of the tall? Probably not. The most famous dinosaur collector active today is James Jensen of Utah. He recently discovered in western Colorado a shoulder blade of unprecedented proportions: nine feet long! He calls its owner *Ultrasaurus*. It seems to resemble Brachiosaurus, and by comparison, it may have stood fifty feet high. If Brachiosaurus weighed forty tons, as is often estimated, Ultrasaurus may have tipped it at a staggering eighty tons!

Ultrasaurus
sauropod
saurischian
herbivore
50 ft. (?)
80 tons (?)
Upper Jurassic
Colorado:
wet and dry
floodplains

Brachiosaurus
sauropod
saurischian
herbivore
40 ft.
40 tons
Upper Jurassic
Colorado Tanzania:
wet and dry
floodplains

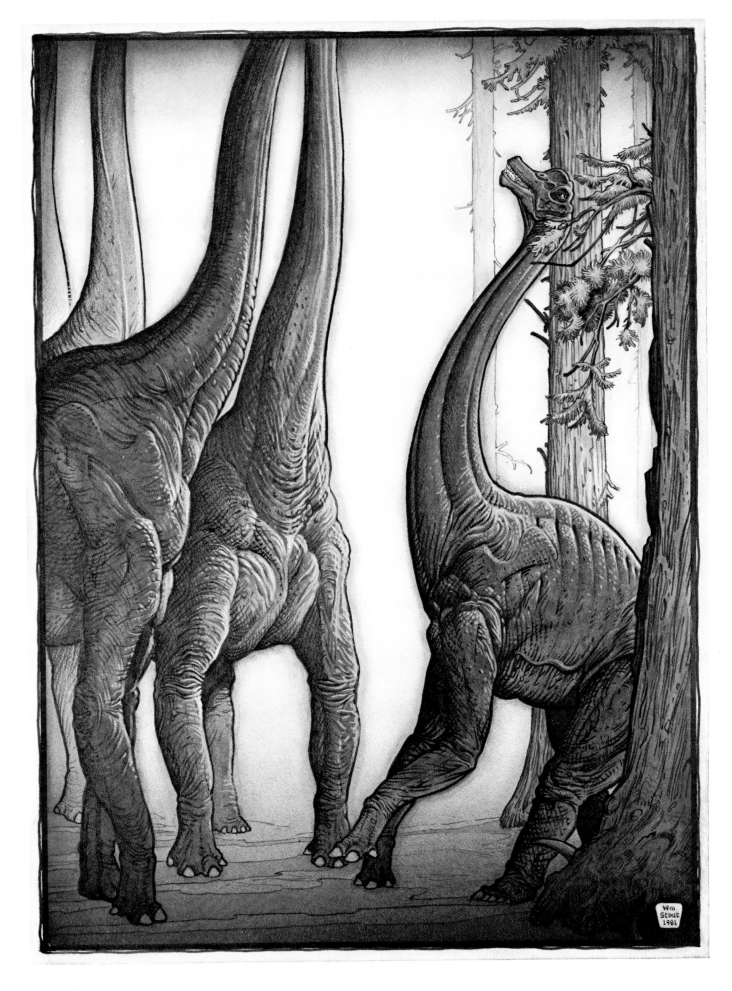

LONGEST

auropods were the biggest of the big. But what do we mean by big? Size can legitimately include linear measurements such as length or height, or a cubic measurement such as weight. Weights of large sauropods strain human intuition to the breaking point. A "small" sauropod, such as a teenage camarasaur, weighed three thousand pounds. Routine estimates of adult sauropod weights range from ten to thirty tons. There is nothing routine about the estimated weight of the large *Brachiosaurus:* forty to fifty-five tons!

Could animals of such weights have walked on land or did they require the support of water to buoy them up? A variety of evidence points to life on land. Sauropods were built like elephants, not like the aquatic hippopotamus. Geological evidence from the western United States where sauropods were very common shows that large bodies of water were uncommon, and that sauropods were buried and preserved in *all* environments, not just those indicating lakes. Although sauropods certainly roamed the waters, they also crossed the land.

Brachiosaurus and *Ultrasaurus* were the

Mamenchisaurus
sauropod
saurischian
herbivore
50-80 ft.
20-30 tons
Upper Jurassic
China:
floodplain

heaviest of dinosaurs, but they were not the longest dinosaurs. Indeed, they were "short-tailed" having a mere fifty-three vertebrae in their tails. *Apatosaurus* and *Diplodocus* were much more bountiful of tail, with more than eighty vertebrae. Their tails ended in a long, slender "whiplash" which added length but very little weight. *Apatosaurus* is often quoted at eighty feet long and *Diplodocus* at nearly ninety feet. Alas, such long, slender, whiplash tails are never found complete. Really large *Apatosaurus* limb bones are known that suggest lengths approaching one hundred feet.

A curious animal is *Mamenchisaurus* from China. It has an enormous pipeline of neck which at thirty feet exceeds that of *Brachiosaurus;* but its limb bones are rather small and suggest at present only a medium size sauropod. The longest dinosaur would be an animal of enormous size that resembled *Diplodocus* in shape. Such an animal, made-to-order, appears to be *Supersaurus.* Evidence of *Supersaurus* was discovered in western Colorado in 1973 by James Jensen. Based on its eight foot shoulder blade, which resembles that of *Diplodocus,* we have an animal which may have been one hundred and twenty-five feet long!

Wm Stout 1981

Ankylosaurus
ankylosaur
ornithischian
herbivore
15 ft.
3 tons
Upper Cretaceous
Alberta, Mongolia:
lowland swamp,
riverbank

WIDEST

T he dinosaurs were fruitful; they went forth, multiplied, and filled the face of the earth. They swarmed across the land, waded in ponds, forded rivers, wallowed in cool mud on hot days, perhaps even swam for the pure fun of it. Dinosaurs were, however, terrestrial animals; that is, they were made for life on land. Their legs were constructed like those of ostriches, rhinoceroses or elephants, not like those of otters, hippos or seals. Another terrestrial feature was the shape of their rib cages. Most dinosaurs had slab chests with long ribs defining a deep, narrow rib cage. This configuration, like that of large land mammals (elephants, giraffes, rhinos), permitted the legs to be relatively close to each other on opposite sides of the body. Even so, in a seventy-foot *Apatosaurus* the rib cage was seven feet wide!

Ankylosaurs, the armored dinosaurs of the Cretaceous, differed from all other kinds of dinosaurs in that they were wide and flat— compressed from top to bottom. *Ankylosaurus magniventris* had a name that literally meant "fused lizard with the great belly." This was an animal that was fifteen or so feet long but more than five feet wide! Like armadillos, and like the extinct mammals called glyptodonts, ankylosaurs carried heavy armor around on their broad backs and ate soft plants growing close to the ground.

FAMILY FACES

SAURISCHIA

In terms of biological classification, dinosaurs all belonged to the same subclass of reptiles: the archosaurs. Dinosaurs belonged to two Orders: the saurischian and the ornithischian. These were distinguished primarily by the structures of the pelvic bones of the dinosaurs. Those with "lizard-hipped" structures were saurischians; those with "bird-hipped" structures were ornithischians. Saurischians and ornithischians also differed in location of teeth and the size of the holes in their skulls behind their eyes. (The holes in saurischian skulls housed jaw muscles which were smaller or non-existant in ornithischians.) Within the saurischian and ornithischian orders, there were subgroups. Saurischia included the suborder theropoda (including the smaller *infraorders* coelurosauria, carnosauria and prosauropoda); and the suborder sauropoda. Ornithischia included the suborders ornithopoda, stegosauria, ankylosauria and ceratopsia.

Within each suborder and infraorder were the different dinosaur *families,* and within each family, the various related *genera* of dinosaur.

On the following pages are the portraits of a wide variety of saurischians and ornithischians, including their *order, family* and *genus.*

Additional information about the biological classification of dinosaurs, can be found in the *Paleontology Primer* in the back of this book.

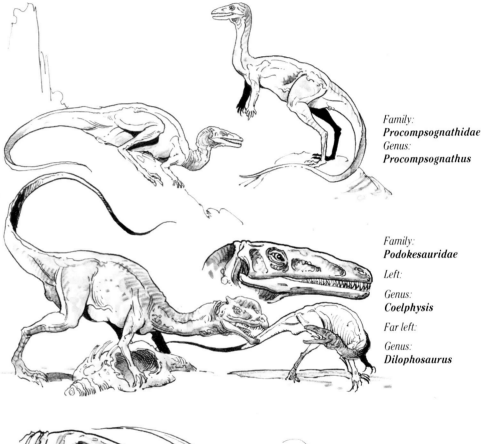

Family:
Procompsognathidae
Genus:
Procompsognathus

Family:
Podokesauridae

Left:

Genus:
Coelphysis

Far left:

Genus:
Dilophosaurus

Family:
Shanshanosauridae
Genus:
Shanshanosaurus

Family:
Compsognathidae
Genus:
Compsognathus

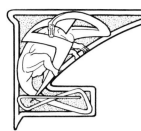 

SAURISCHIA

Family:
Segisauridae
Genus:
Segisaurus
*(known only
by its claws)*

Family:
Coeluridae
Genus:
Ornitholestes

Family:
Segnosauridae
Genus:
Erlikosaurus

SAURISCHIA

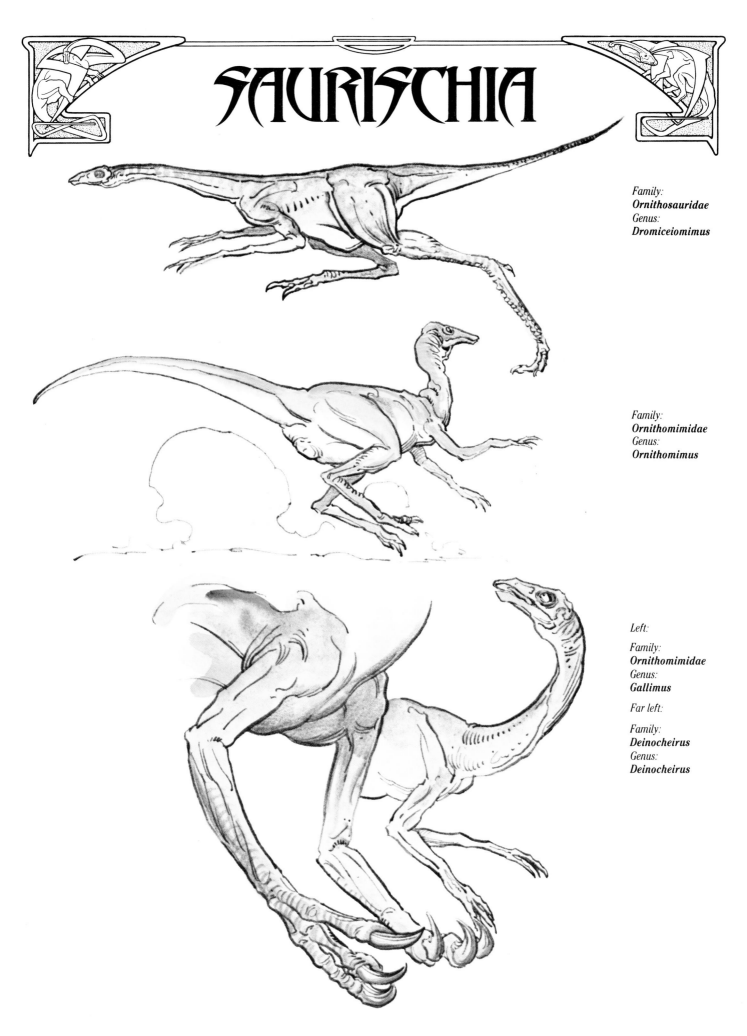

Family:
Ornithosauridae
Genus:
Dromiceiomimus

Family:
Ornithomimidae
Genus:
Ornithomimus

Left:

Family:
Ornithomimidae
Genus:
Gallimus

Far left:

Family:
Deinocheirus
Genus:
Deinocheirus

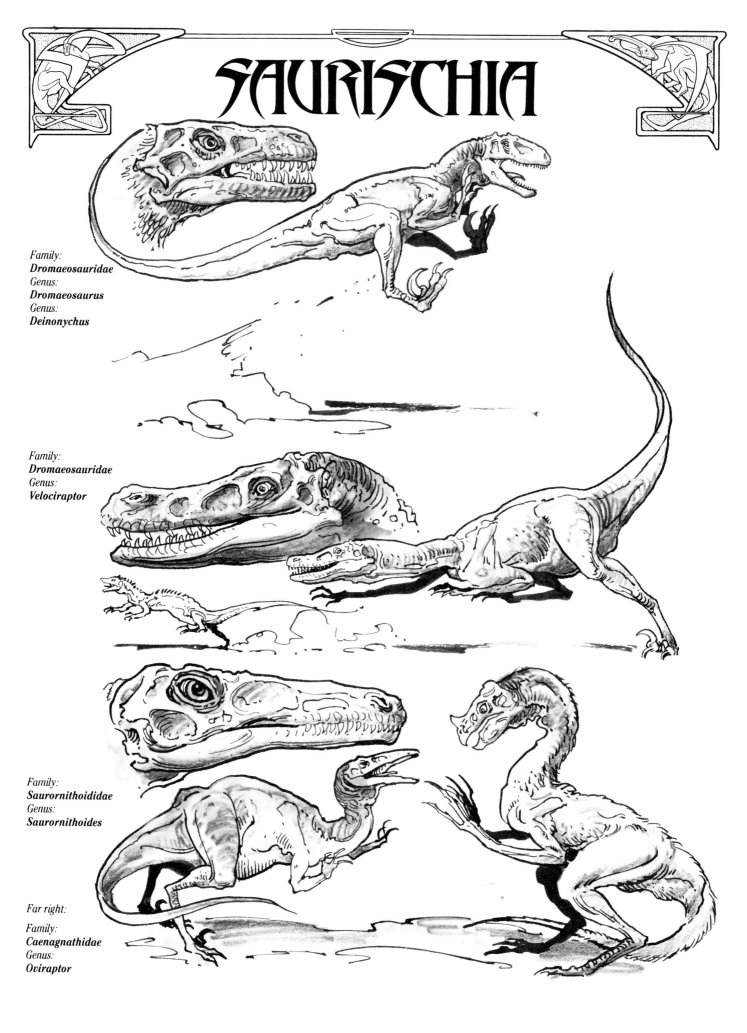

SAURISCHIA

Family:
Dromaeosauridae
Genus:
Dromaeosaurus
Genus:
Deinonychus

Family:
Dromaeosauridae
Genus:
Velociraptor

Family:
Saurornithoididae
Genus:
Saurornithoides

Far right:
Family:
Caenagnathidae
Genus:
Oviraptor

SAURISCHIA

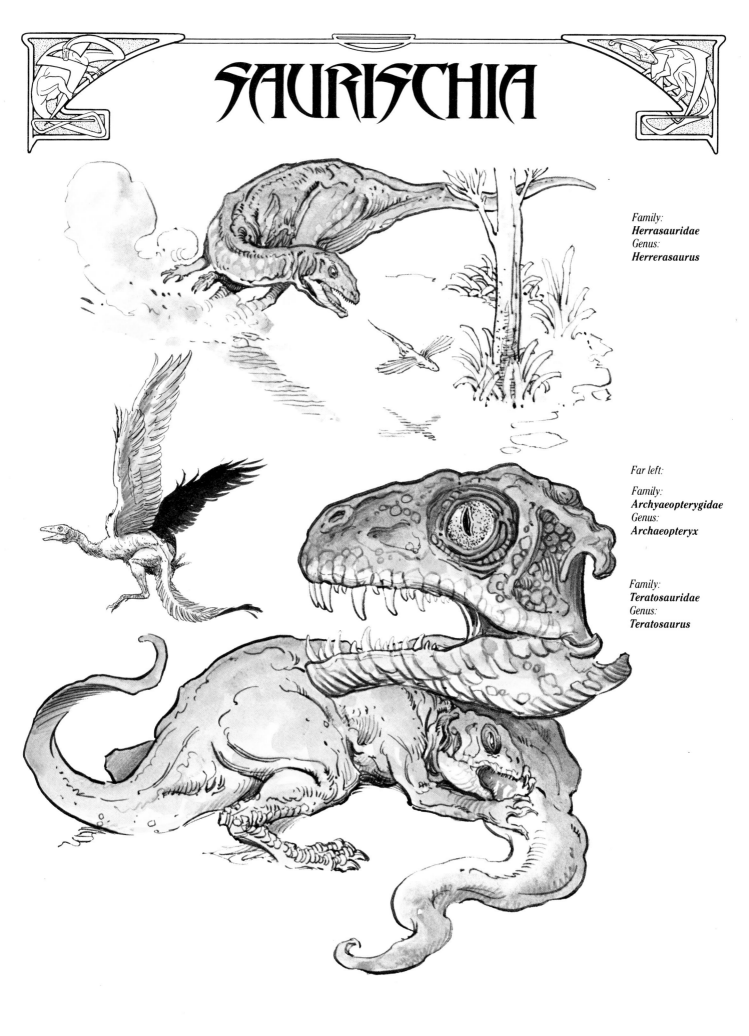

Family:
Herrasauridae
Genus:
Herrerasaurus

Far left:

Family:
Archyaeopterygidae
Genus:
Archaeopteryx

Family:
Teratosauridae
Genus:
Teratosaurus

SAURISCHIA

Family:
Megalosauridae
Genus:
Megalosaurus

Family:
Allosauridae
Genus:
Allosaurus

Family:
Ceratosauridae
Genus:
Ceratosaurus

SAURISCHIA

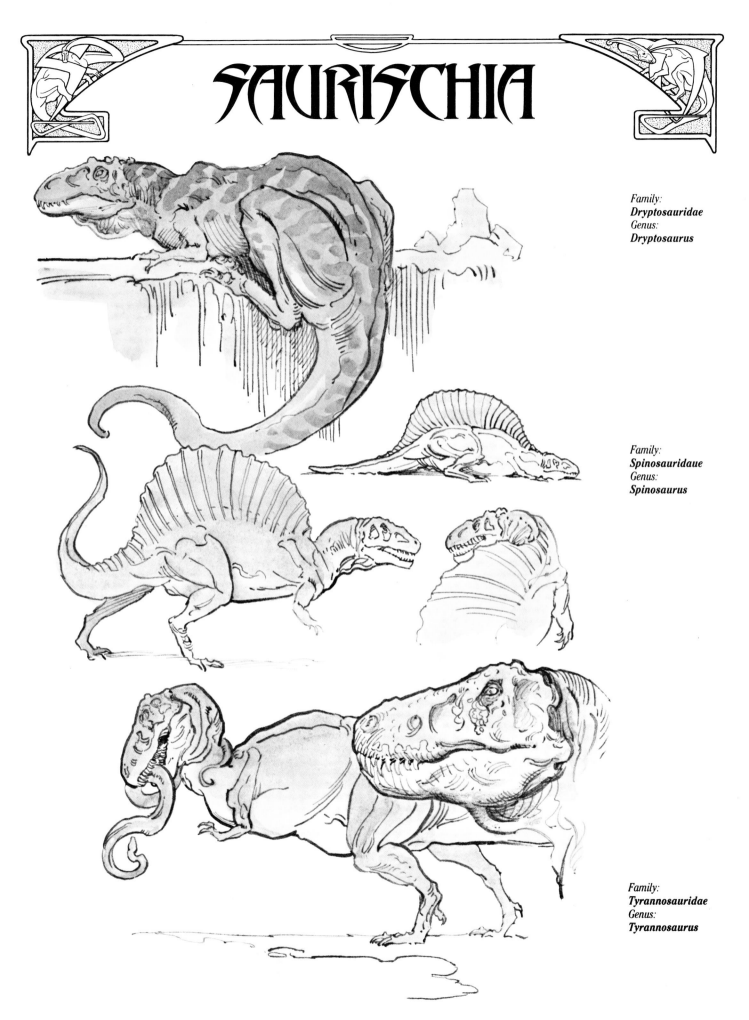

Family:
Dryptosauridae
Genus:
Dryptosaurus

Family:
Spinosauridaue
Genus:
Spinosaurus

Family:
Tyrannosauridae
Genus:
Tyrannosaurus

SAURISCHIA

Family:
Therizinosauridae
Genus:
Chilantaisauras

Family:
Anchisauridae
Genus:
Anchisauras
Genus:
Efraasia

Family:
Staurikosauridae
Genus:
Staurikosaurus

SAURISCHIA

Family:
Plateosauridae
Genus:
Plateosaurus

Family:
Melanosauridae
Genus:
Melanosaurus

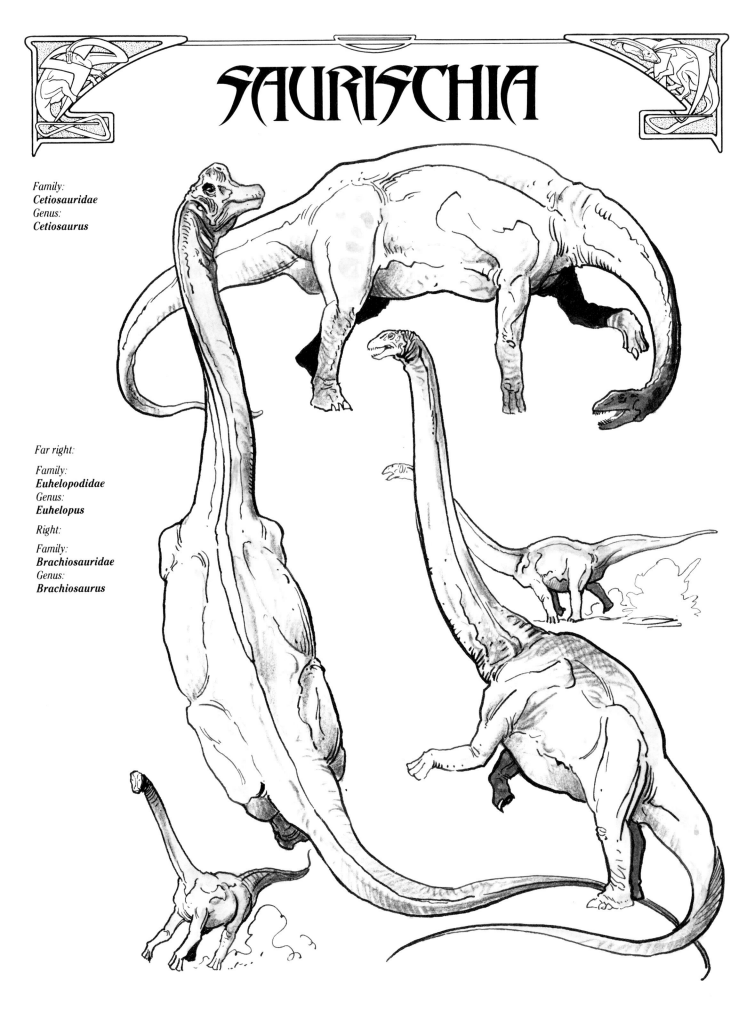

SAURISCHIA

Family:
Cetiosauridae
Genus:
Cetiosaurus

Far right:

Family:
Euhelopodidae
Genus:
Euhelopus

Right:

Family:
Brachiosauridae
Genus:
Brachiosaurus

SAURISCHIA

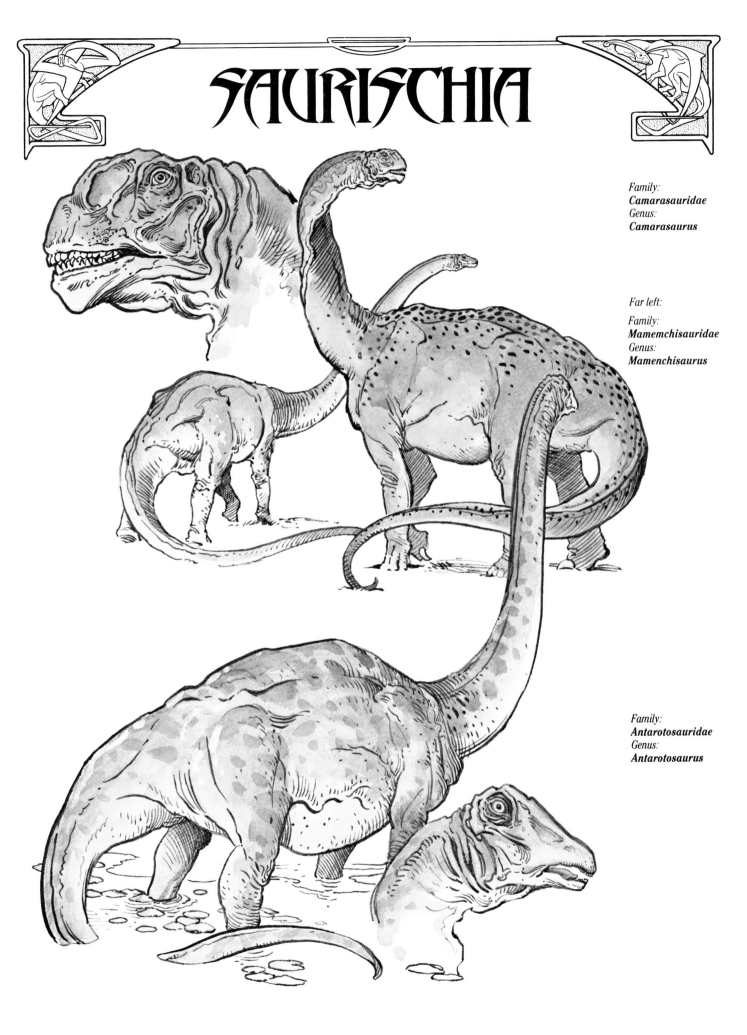

Family:
Camarasauridae
Genus:
Camarasaurus

Far left:
Family:
Mamemchisauridae
Genus:
Mamenchisaurus

Family:
Antarotosauridae
Genus:
Antarotosaurus

SAURISCHIA

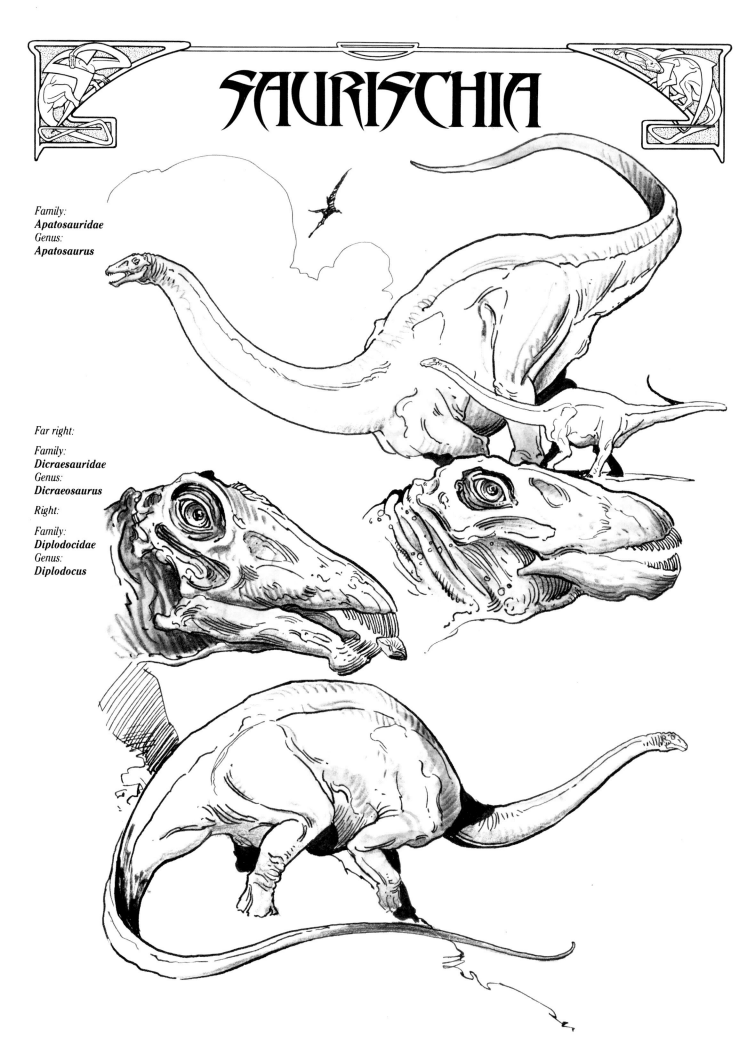

Family:
Apatosauridae
Genus:
Apatosaurus

Far right:

Family:
Dicraesauridae
Genus:
Dicraeosaurus

Right:

Family:
Diplodocidae
Genus:
Diplodocus

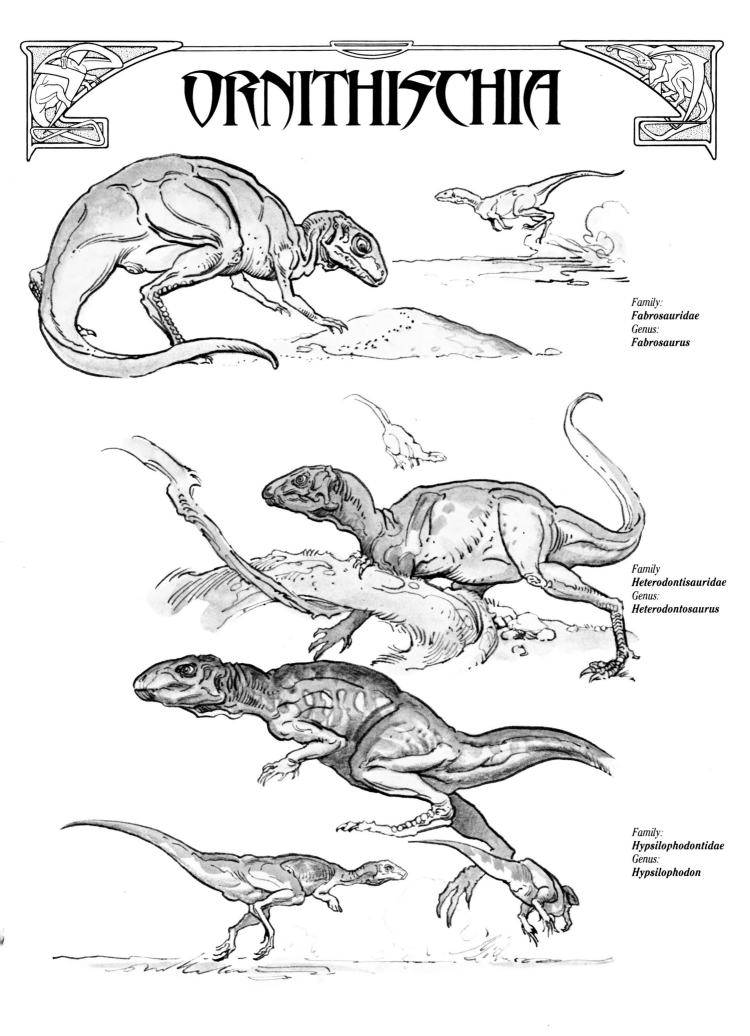

ORNITHISCHIA

Family:
Fabrosauridae
Genus:
Fabrosaurus

Family
Heterodontisauridae
Genus:
Heterodontosaurus

Family:
Hypsilophodontidae
Genus:
Hypsilophodon

ORNITHISCHIA

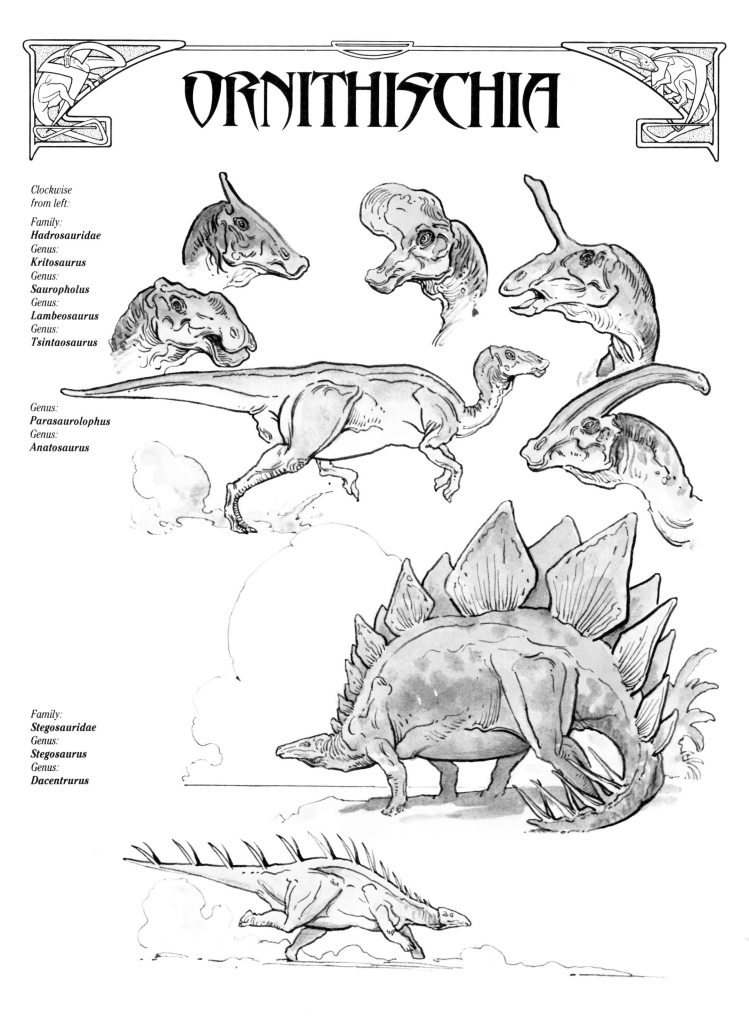

*Clockwise
from left:*

Family:
Hadrosauridae
Genus:
Kritosaurus
Genus:
Sauropholus
Genus:
Lambeosaurus
Genus:
Tsintaosaurus

Genus:
Parasaurolophus
Genus:
Anatosaurus

Family:
Stegosauridae
Genus:
Stegosaurus
Genus:
Dacentrurus

ORNITHISCHIA

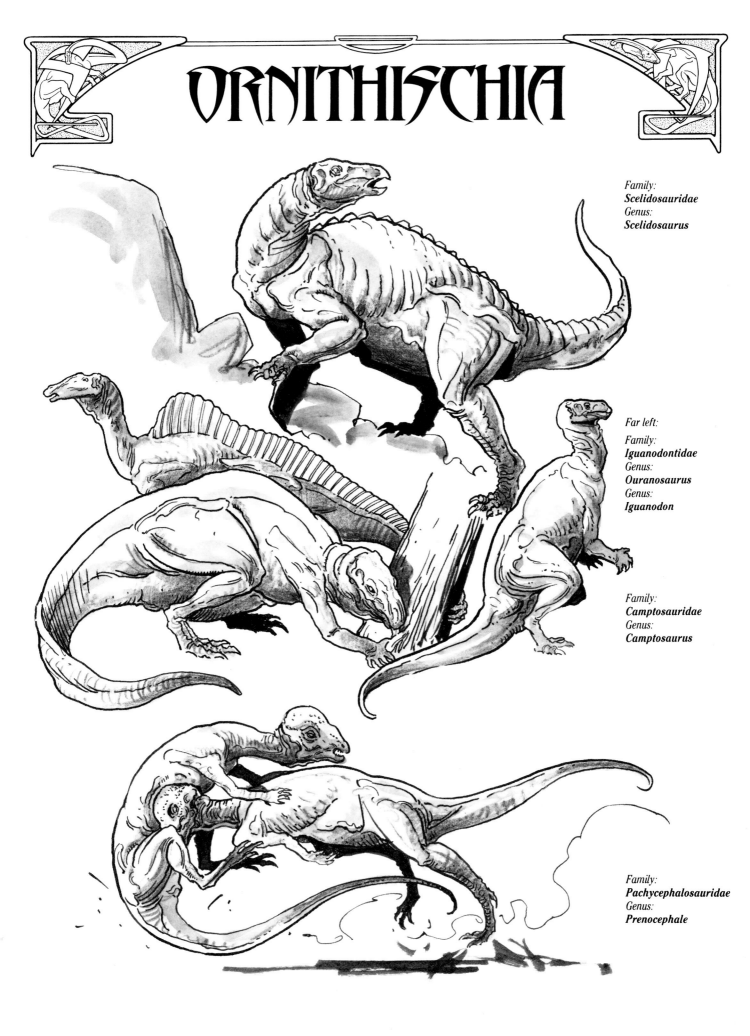

Family:
Scelidosauridae
Genus:
Scelidosaurus

Far left:
Family:
Iguanodontidae
Genus:
Ouranosaurus
Genus:
Iguanodon

Family:
Camptosauridae
Genus:
Camptosaurus

Family:
Pachycephalosauridae
Genus:
Prenocephale

ORNITHISCHIA

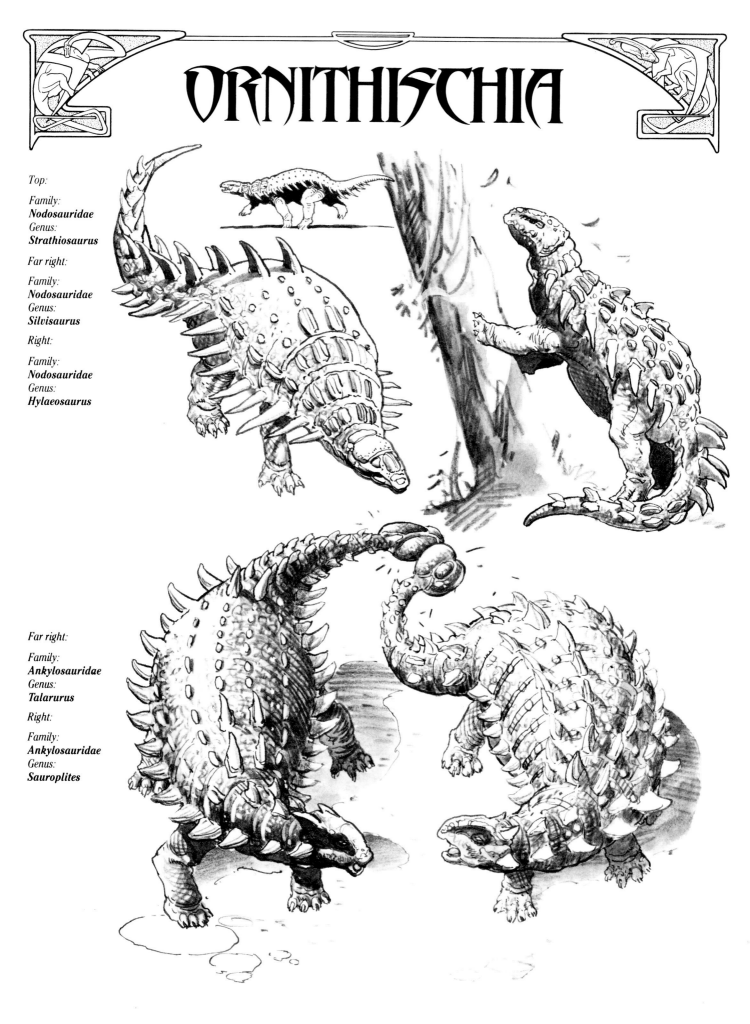

Top:

Family:
Nodosauridae
Genus:
Strathiosaurus

Far right:

Family:
Nodosauridae
Genus:
Silvisaurus

Right:

Family:
Nodosauridae
Genus:
Hylaeosaurus

Far right:

Family:
Ankylosauridae
Genus:
Talarurus

Right:

Family:
Ankylosauridae
Genus:
Sauroplites

ORNITHISCHIA

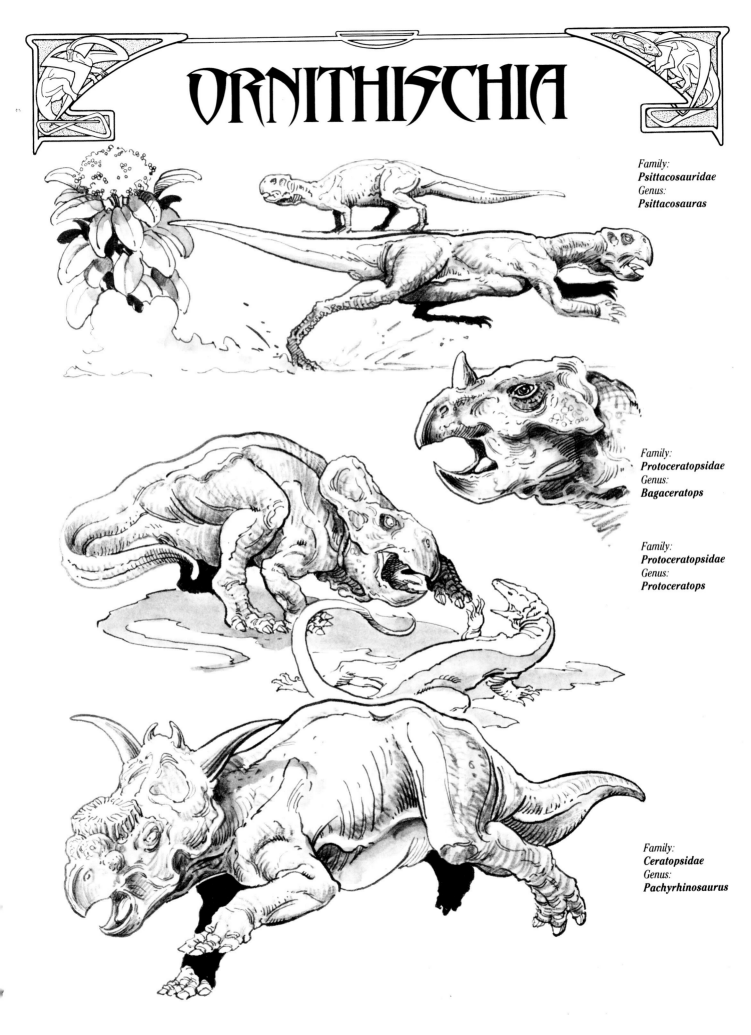

Family:
Psittacosauridae
Genus:
Psittacosauras

Family:
Protoceratopsidae
Genus:
Bagaceratops

Family:
Protoceratopsidae
Genus:
Protoceratops

Family:
Ceratopsidae
Genus:
Pachyrhinosaurus

ENDANGERED SPECIES

T he archosaurs are mostly gone now, dropped out of the sky, sunk to the bottom, fallen to the ground . . . dissolved or buried. So too the trilobites and myriad species of insects known only from their etchings in fine-grained rock. Recently gone are the mammoth, the auk, the forest buffalo. Soon to go, if not protected, are most of the creatures designated "endangered species": right whale, California condor, black-foot ferret. . . . And yet, every species now alive faces "extinction" with an inevitability of something like one out of one, and only hedging forbids putting it *exactly* one out of one. Final cataclysm need not be the agent: for every species, the eons will prove just as final. In a million years, our own successors—if any— will consider us as extinct as we consider the Australopithecines. In the same span, mastodon and elephant, hyracotherium and horse may go through the same process. Such is the orderly, the benign aspect of evolution— a species, gradually or suddenly replaced by it own progeny as life adjusts to changes in its world, as life competes with life.

The disappearances of great classes and orders of life from the face of the earth, on the other hand, present something enigmat-

ic and ominous . . . a *memento mori* which both demands and eludes comprehension. Compared to those disappearances, the man-made extinctions of species seem merely disgusting sequences for which it is necessary only to sort out and fit together the links: slaughter, poison, destruction of habitat, human hunger and cold greed, imported enemies, greed, ignorance, poverty, shortsightedness, indifference, greed. In both types of disappearances however, a form of life has been condemned to die without issue. Should humanity be willing, in greed and indifference, to assign to itself nature's awesome power of condemnation?

In the natural disappearances, whether as massive as the dinosaurs' or as slight as that of the little understory tree, *Franklinia,* which today lives on only in gardens, arboretums, and nurseries, we confront the enigma. We can list the factors which must work, singly or in combination, to eradicate a species: predator pressure, competition, climatic change, etc. The list could be extended and the categories refined without generating much enlightenment. The fact is, no natural extinction—that long equation which ends up equalling zero—has been completely solved in terms of those factors.

1. Walrus 2. Sea Otter 3. Hawksbill Turtle 4. Blue Whale (larger than any dinosaur) 5. Gavial 6. Manatee 7. Slender Salamander 8. Galapagos Penguin 9. Northern Elephant Seal 10. Marine Iguana

We can only speculate.

Consider the concept, *fitness*, as in survival-of-the-fittest. We do not know how to assign the quality to any species in and of itself. Certainly the ichthyosaur, who jumped and plunged through Triassic and Jurassic seas, a marine reptile as powerfully and elegantly shaped as the modern porpoise, would appear "fit". Fading out in the early Cretaceous, it disappeared long before lumbering old titanosaur did. The camel throve in the savannahs of North America, radiated to other continents . . . and disappeared from North America. The troublesome intangible is this: The spider's survival depends on the fly's—figuratively speaking, for many species of spider rarely, if ever, encounter a fly—and the wasp's survival depends on the spider's—literally speaking, because many species of wasp have no other food for themselves or for their larvae. But if the dainty parasitic wasps who live on the larvae of the spider-eating wasps, and keep their numbers down, die off, will the spiders survive? Man, being an omnivore, hopes not to depend on niceties such as that.

With some deceptive sense of security, then, we can contemplate extinctions in their various forms. Just as we assign degrees to murder and distinguish it from manslaughter and from capital punishment, so we can distinguish different kinds of extinction. Hyracotherium, for example, and the mastodon, are gone, but in a genetic sense live on through their respective descendants, horse and elephant. Indeed, the competition from their only slightly altered progeny may have led to their own demise.

The sabre-tooth cats, who no longer menace us, apparently have no direct descendants, yet close collateral lines throng our zoos and homes. The surviving collateral lines of the prodigious ground sloth and of the sabre-tooth marsupials seem a degree more removed from their forebears, whether clinging in diminished numbers from limbs of tropical trees or thronging the plains of Australia, or, as possum, exploiting the vegetable gardens and garbage cans of the eastern United States. (A very different perspective, viewed through the cold eye of the jawless fish who preceded us all, from man to lamprey eel, less than two billion years ago, identifies us as all one spawn in whose midst the difference between dead dinosaur and living primate is slight.) Which leaves the so-called great extinctions, the disappearance of entire orders which died without issue. Among them, the trilobites, who scuttled or paddled through the waters a truly long time ago, as far as life is reckoned, whose humble adaptability and determined multiplicity, as with pigeons and roaches, would seem to have ensured some kind of lock on life. Among them also our Mesozoic coelurosaurs, who moved quickly and ate what they could snatch up, not demanding monstrous feasts of red meat. In addition, the great carnosaurs, who seemed able to enforce any such demands they might make. No flora or fauna seems exempt from some kind of extinction, not soaring pteranodon nor any kind of marine or terrestrial mollusk, nor tree, nor weed, nor insect. The questions are what kind, when and how. If the

1. Indigo Macaw 2. Cock-of-the-rock 3. Monkey-eating Eagle 4. Nene Goose 5. Japanese Crested Ibis 6. California Condor 7. White-eared Pheasant 8. Southern Bald Eagle 9. Great Indian Hornbill 10. White-necked Rock Fowl 11. Mississippi Sandhill Crane

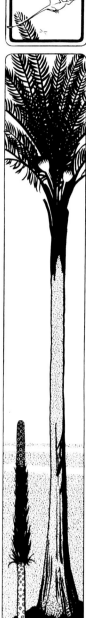

proper steps are not taken, the likely answer for one, two or all of the following may be, soon, and, by our own actions: blue whale, salmon, falcon, rhinoceros, mountain gorilla, desert pupfish. We would not be materially threatened for the loss of any. Our exterminations, not only of dozens of other species, but—attempted or achieved— of our own races and tribes have sadly, conditioned us to act with impunity. Nevertheless, the loss would still be felt: the loss of beauty, of interaction, and diversity. It is this impoverishment of our world which we must respond to.

What practical difference would it have made had the last American buffalo perished? What practical difference does it make that, decade by decade, not only is the rate of extinction increasing, but the total mass of life on earth, through man's operations, is diminishing? One cautionary answer, one reservation, one *caveat* persists: A disappearance tells us each time that some terrain has been spoiled, that some way of surviving has been rubbed out. A creature which poisons its own waters, reduces its forests to sources of pulp and material for carpentry, and flushes away its own productive ground must be marching into some kind of jeopardy. The planet's tectonic plates heave up fresh rocks too slowly, the weather grinds them into earth too slowly, the living waters purge themselves of our poisons too slowly for the pace of our ambitions. Unfortunately for the lesson, although fortunately for our prosperity, the consequences also will arrive too slowly. We hack away, not at our own sub-

1. Ruffed Lemur 2. Orangutan 3. Giant Anteater 4. Polar Bear 5. Marbled Cat 6. Black Rhino 7. Lowland Gorilla 8. Wolf 9. Rhea 10. Maned Wolf 11. Snow Leopard 12. Mountain Tapir 13. Tuatara

strate, nor probably even at our children's, but at the substrate of remote generations.

Assume, now, that we have decided to control ambition and to desist from ripping and fouling the earth's mantle. We turn our attention to the various endangered species, one by one. We find, ironically, that it is not the harpooner of whales, the clubber of fur seals, the poacher of rhinos who has the power and the means to save those animals—in most such cases, they are his immediate livelihood. It falls on the society which elects to preserve, for example, the fur seal, to fulfill a two-fold responsibility: First, to choose something else to make an evening wrap out of; second, to develop an alternate means of livelihood for the men the society originally hired to club them.

The mite infests only the left ear of the bat: To infest both would upset the bat's echolocation of flying insects and so diminish the fortunes of his passenger mite. Such precision of interdependence of life is as awesome as the execution of an entire family of marine reptiles— creatures as formidable as sharks or killer whales. Pteranodon falls, roach rises . . . In trying to contemplate this mighty scheme, we are children. We have only started to understand the factors that bind all life together.

Out of respect for that life, out of respect for what is only the dawning of our understanding of its complexity, what could be more fitting than for humanity to recognize that to protect other life forms is to protect our own life on this planet.

A PALEONTOLOGY PRIMER

by Dr. Peter Dodson

GLOSSARY[†]

advanced highly evolved

amphibian limbed, cold-blooded *vertebrates* with moist skin who change from gill-breathing larvae to air-breathing adults

angiosperm modern flowering plant with seeds enclosed in ovary

archaic little evolved, close to condition of ancestors

archeology scientific study of humanity's past life and culture by analysis of their artifacts, records, structures and other remains

archosaur the *subclass* of *reptiles* that includes *crocodiles, dinosaurs, pterosaurs,* and their ancestors

biped animal that walks on two legs

bird *warm-blooded,* feathered, egg-laying *vertebrate* usually capable of flying

carnivore animal that eats meat

class* major subdivision of life, usually consisting of several *orders;* ex.: *reptiles, birds, mammals*

cold-blooded pertaining to animals whose temperatures vary in accordance with the temperature of the environment

conservative slow to evolve

Cretaceous last of three periods of the Age of Reptiles—135 to 63 million years ago

crocodilian the sole surviving *order* of *archosaurs:* amphibious *predators* including alligators, caimans, crocodiles and gavials

cycad group of palm-like *gymnosperms* common in the *Mesozoic* but still in existence today

delta deposit formed where river meets a lake or an ocean

dinosaur *archosaur* belonging either to the Order *Saurischia* or the Order *Ornithischia*

ectotherm animal that derives its body heat from an external source, as by basking in the sun; ex.: all living *reptiles*

endotherm animal that derives body heat from internal *metabolism;* ex. all modern *birds* and *mammals*

evolution biological process of descent with modification through time

extinction termination of a *species*

family* a group of related *genera*

femur thigh bone

floodplain area periodically flooded by a river

fossil remains of ancient life

genus* a division consisting of one or more *species* differing only in minor details; ex.: horses and zebras are of the same genus, Equus. The plural of genus is *genera*

gingko maidenhair tree, broad-leafed *gymnosperm* of the *Mesozoic Era* that still exists today

gymnosperm the array of seed plants that includes *cycads* and conifers (pines, spruces, etc.)

herbivore animal that eats plants

homeotherm animal that has constant body temperature—as do most *birds* and *mammals*

humerus bone of the upper arm

ilium upper bone of the hip

ischium hip bone projecting down and back

Jurassic the middle period of the Age of Reptiles—190 to 140 million years ago

lower referring to rocks more distant from the present

mammal *warm-blooded,* furred *vertebrate* that suckles its live-born young (except monotremes, the lowest *order* of *mammals,* who lay eggs)

Mesozoic Era the Age of Reptiles, comprising *Triassic, Jurassic* and *Cretaceous* periods

metabolism the chemical process of life by which food is made available to the organism for maintenance, growth and activity

modern resembling condition characteristic of presently living organisms

order a group of *families* that share a number of common features

ornithischia the *order* of plant-eating, bird-hipped *dinosaurs*

paleontology the study of *fossils,* the remains of ancient life, including *dinosaurs*

plesiosaur a marine *reptile* with paddles, totally unrelated to *dinosaurs*

poikilotherm animal whose body temperature varies during the day; ex.: lizards

predator a meat-eater that hunts its prey

primitive resembling the condition characteristic of ancestors, or organisms ancestral to kinds who followed

pterosaur flying archosaur, cousin of dinosaurs

pubis hip bone projecting down and forward in *saurischians*

quadruped animal that walks on four legs

reptile *cold-blooded,* scale-covered, egg-laying *vertebrate*

saurischia the *order* of reptile-hipped *dinosaurs* that includes meat-eaters and plant-eaters

scapula long blade-like bone of the shoulder girdle

scavenger animal that obtains its meat from carrion

sediment particles of material deposited from water or air

sophisticated possessing complex, highly-evolved features

species* a group of organisms that share the same genes through interbreeding. (The singular and plural of species are the same.)

stratigraphy the study of strata, or beds of rock, to determine age

subclass* a division of a *class* consisting of groups of related *orders;* ex. one subclass of *reptiles* includes *archosaurs,* another lizards

suborder* a division of an *order* consisting of a group of related *families;* ex. one suborder of *Saurischia* includes sauropods, the other theropods

taxonomy the arranging of *species* into higher groups

thecodont *order* of primitive *archosaurs* from which *dinosaurs* arose

therapsid *order* of reptiles that gave rise to true *mammals*

tibia major bone of the calf or lower leg

Triassic first of the three periods of the Age of Reptiles—225 to 190 million years ago

upper referring to rocks closer in time to the present

vertebrate animal possessing a backbone and a brain enclosed in a skull or cranium with a special plan of organization

warm-blooded pertaining to animals whose blood temperature remains relatively constant irrespective of the surrounding environment

Ornithischian hip-bones

illium

pubis   *ischium*

"bird-hipped"

Iguanadon is an ornithischian.

Saurischian hip-bones

illium

pubis   *ischium*

"lizard-hipped"

Tyrannosaurus is a saurischian.

[†]*All italicized words are defined in this glossary.*

**Refer to Classification chart on the following page.*

CLASSIFICATION

A system of biological classification is the systematic organization of organisms into a coherent order which expresses both the anatomical and evolutionary relationships between them.

Categories of biological classification in descending order of comprehensiveness are: *kingdom, phylum* (division), *class, subclass, order, suborder, infraorder, family, genus,* and *species.*

Dinosaurs belong to the

Kingdom: Animalia
Phylum: Chordata
Class: Reptilia (the debated relationship between dinosaurs and avians has caused this classification to be the subject of controversy among some paleontologists)

Subclass: Archosauria
Order: Saurischia, including the *suborder* Sauropodomorpha (including the *infraorders* sauropoda and prosauropoda) and the *suborder* therapoda (including the *infraorders* coelurosauria and carnosauria)
Order: Ornithischia, including the *suborders* ornithopoda, stegosauria, ankylosauria and ceratopsia
Families: such as the hadrosaurs and the stegosaurs
Genera: such as the parasaurolophus and kentrosaurus of the hadrosaur and stegosaur family, respectively
Species: such as the parasaurolophus walkeri (named for its discoverer) and kentosaurus aethiopius, respectively.

CHRONOLOGY

	TRIASSIC	LOWER JURASSIC	UPPER JURASSIC	LOWER CRETACEOUS	UPPER CRETACEOUS
Saurischia					
coelurosaur			Coelurus Ornitholestes	Deinonychus	Velociraptor Dromaeosaurus
ornithomimid					Dromiceiomimus
carnosaur		Megalosaurus	Allosaurus Ceratosaurus		Albertosaurus Alioramus Daspletosaurus Dryptosaurus Spinosaurus Tyrannosaurus
sauropod			Apatosaurus Brachiosaurus Camarasaurus Diplodocus Haplocanthosaurus Mamenchisaurus Ultrasaurus		Alamosaurus Laplatasaurus
Ornithischia					
ornithopod	Fabrosaurus Heterodontosaurus	Callovosaurus Scelidosaurus	Camptosaurus Dryosaurus Othnielia	Hypsilophodon Iguanodon Tenontosaurus	Parksosaurus Psittacosaurus
pachycephalosaur					Homalocephale Pachycephalosaurus
hadrosaur					Anatosaurus Brachylophosaurus Corythosaurus Hadrosaurus Lambeosaurus Parasaurolophus Prosaurolphus Saurolophus
stegosaur			Kentrosaurus Stegosaurus		
ankylosaur					Ankylosaurus Euplocephalus Tarchia
ceratopsian					Anchiceratops Centrosaurus Chasmosaurus Monoclonius Pachyrhinosaurs Protoceratops Styracosaurus Torosaurus Triceratops

225 MILLION YEARS AGO   193 MILLION YEARS AGO   136 MILLION YEARS AGO   63 MILLION YEARS AGO

GEOGRAPHY

Africa
Brachiosaurus*
Ceratosaurus*
Dryosaurus*
Fabrosaurus
Heterodontosaurus
Kentrosaurus
Laplatasaurus
Spinosaurus
Syntarsus

Asia
Alioramus
Homalocephale
Laplatasaurus
Longisquama*
Mamenchisaurus
Protoceratops
Saurolophus*
Tarchia
Velociraptor
Psittacosaurus

Europe
Archaeopteryx*
Callovosaurus
Camptosaurus*
Hypsilophodon
Iguanodon
Megalosaurus
Scelidosaurus
Ticinosuchus

North America
All other animals featured on these two pages and all animals in the adjacent columns with an asterisk lived in areas that are now part of North America.

South America
Dinodontosaurus*
Gracilisuchus*
Lagosuchus*
Laplatasaurus

Statistics in this chart and the others are subject to change based on new discoveries and reinterpretation of existing evidence.

HEIGHTS

Ultrasaurus 50 ft. "Ultrasaurus" is not yet an established name. Statistics regarding its total size, weight and height have not been established.

50	
45	
40	**Brachiosaurus** 40 ft.
35	**Mamenchisaurus** 35 ft. The skeleton of *mamemchisaurus*, as preserved, without the back of its tail, is just over 62 feet long.
30	
25	**Camarasaurus** 25 ft.
20	
	Iguanodon 18 ft.
15	**Corythosaurus** 15 ft.

A large *hypsilophodon* may have stood over six feet tall. An adult *compsognathus* may have been as tall as two feet.

Tenontosaurus 10 ft. — 10
Dryosaurus 7 ft.
Ankylosaurus 5 ft. — 5 — **Hypsilophodon** 3 ft.
Compsognathus 1 ft.
Syntarsus 2 ft.
Psittacosaurus (baby) 3 in. — 0

feet

WEIGHTS

This chart includes ranges of weights where series of specimens are known. William Morris has unearthed evidence of *lambeosaurs* that may have been 50 feet long and up to 15 tons in weight.

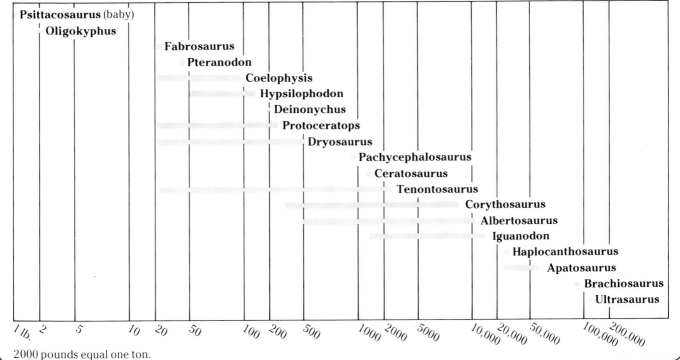

Psittacosaurus (baby)
Oligokyphus
Fabrosaurus
Pteranodon
Coelophysis
Hypsilophodon
Deinonychus
Protoceratops
Dryosaurus
Pachycephalosaurus
Ceratosaurus
Tenontosaurus
Corythosaurus
Albertosaurus
Iguanodon
Haplocanthosaurus
Apatosaurus
Brachiosaurus
Ultrasaurus

1 lb. 2 5 10 20 50 100 200 500 1000 2000 5000 10,000 20,000 50,000 100,000 200,000

2000 pounds equal one ton.

ABOUT THE CONTRIBUTORS

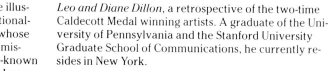

WILLIAM STOUT, the illustrator, is an internationally acclaimed artist whose work has been commissioned by such well-known directors as George Lucas and John Milius, for whom he has produced poster and production designs respectively. As an illustrator of prehistoric life, he held his first one-man show in Los Angeles in 1977, and won the enthusiasm of paleontologists and fantasy lovers alike. His illustrations of dinosaurs have been featured in Donald Glut's *Dinosaur Dictionary*, *The Dinosaur Scrapbook*, and in a limited full color portfolio. In the summer of 1981, Stout was one of a handful of dinosaur artists featured in a major exhibition at Los Angeles' Griffith Observatory. Stout is an avid reader of paleontological research and meets regularly with students of the Mesozoic Era to discuss new findings. Stout first won acclaim for his underground record covers and comics; the former were the subject of a retrospective in the French magazine, *Metal Hurlant*. He has produced posters for such films as *More American Graffiti*, *Rock and Roll High School*, *Wizards* and *Allegro Non Troppo* and did production design for *Buck Rogers*. Stout collaborated with the Firesign Theatre on the graphics for their film, *Everything You Know is Wrong* and illustrated the cover of their album, *In the Next World You're On Your Own*. He has also produced album graphics for the Beach Boys, Rhino Records, and a line of film score records. He holds a B.A. from the Chouinard Art Institute (the California Institute of the Arts) and has had his work published in England, Australia, Spain, France, Italy and the United States. He currently resides in Hollywood.

WILLIAM SERVICE, author, is a graduate of Princeton University. His book, *Owl*, currently published by Penguin Books, was called "one of the most elegant and perceptive pieces of nature writing since T.H. White fell in love with a goshawk" by *Time* Magazine, and "a delightful read" by the *Chicago Tribune*. Considered a classic of its kind, it has earned Service a circle of fans in the United States. A contributor to *Sports Illustrated*, he currently resides in Efland, North Carolina with his wife Pegge, a director of language laboratories at Duke University.

BYRON PREISS, editor, is the co-author and producer of Bantam's bestselling trade paperback, *Dragonworld*, of which Maurice Sendak said, "Dragonworld goes far beyond the flashy pyrotechnics of contemporary fantasy and fantasy illustration." Preiss is considered to be one of the major figures in the renaissance of illustrated fiction in America. He has written for the Children's Television Workshop and ABC-TV. He is the author of the authorized biography of The Beach Boys and *The Art of*

Leo and Diane Dillon, a retrospective of the two-time Caldecott Medal winning artists. A graduate of the University of Pennsylvania and the Stanford University Graduate School of Communications, he currently resides in New York.

PETER DODSON Ph.D., the scientific consultant, studied paleontology at Yale University under the direction of John Ostrom. The author of more than 20 scientific publications, he exemplifies the modern approach to paleontology. An associate professor of animal biology and teacher of veterinary anatomy at the University of Pennsylvania Veterinary School, he believes that the key to understanding the biology of extinct animals is to understand the biology of relevant models among our living creatures. Thus he works with alligators and owls, and has applied his findings to fossils. He has worked for a number of seasons in the dinosaur beds of western Canada and the United States, and has studied growth series of several species of dinosaurs. He holds three degrees in geology and is co-author, with his father, Edward O. Dodson, of *Evolution, Process and Product*.

DINOSAURS PRINTS

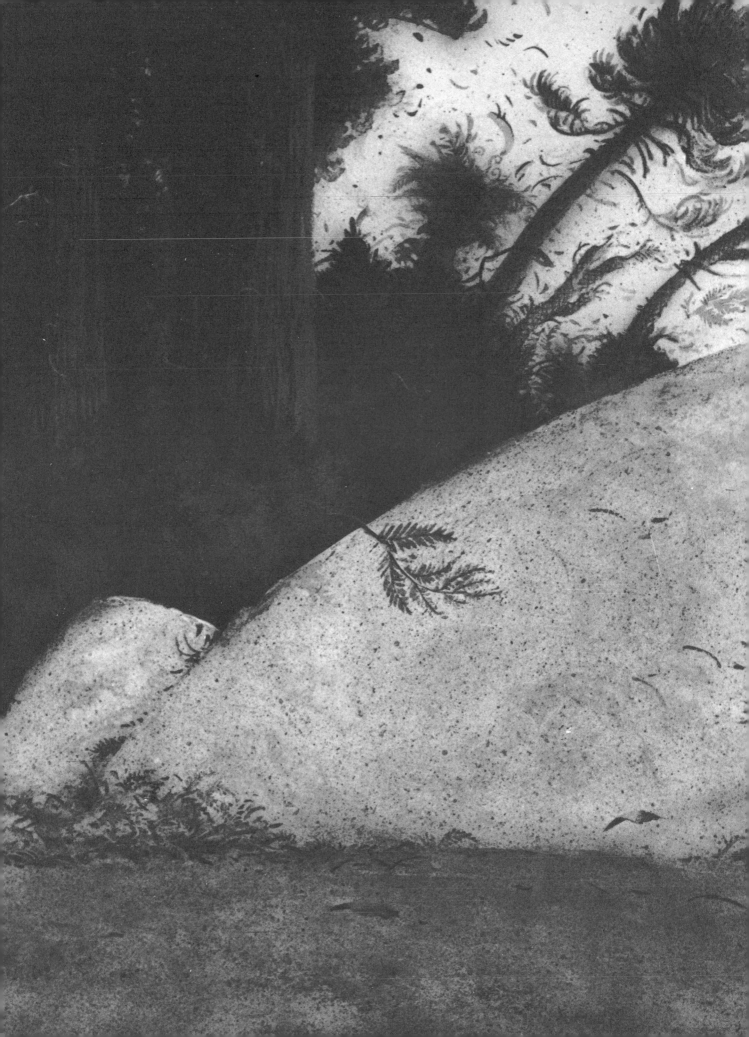